INTRODUCTION

By

(John A Gallagher)

Edmund James Gallagher, my father, wrote a manuscript simply called 'Anticosti'. He never had the manuscript published so I shall try and accomplish that for him. Dad died in 1974 in The Montreal General Hospital of pancreatic cancer, I believe that he would be pleased if I can accomplish that because after all is said and done, I spent the last night of his life on earth with just him and I alone together. He was in bed of course and I was spread out on 3 folding chairs by the side of his bed. I woke up very early in the morning to the death rattle emanating from deep within him.

I was born in Port –Menier, on the western tip of Anticosti Island, in the Saint Lawrence River, on April 11, 1936. The Island is the 90th largest island in the world and the 20th largest island in Canada. The entire island constitutes one municipality officially known as L' Île-d-Anticosti.

The island is twice the size of the province of Prince Edward Island. Its coastline is 500km long, and is rocky and dangerous; offering very little shelter for ships except in Gamache, Ellis and Fox Bays. Anticosti Island became known as the "Cemetery of the Gulf" because of the more than 400 shipwrecks off its coasts.

I remember stories my older sister Eileen told me; about the times the snow was as high as the third story bedroom windows. As the baby, a year and a half old maybe, the older kids like Eileen would sit me in a wooden sleigh with a wood back on it, and there I'd sit all wrapped up warm in blankets as they pushed me out the window and down the hill all by myself. Apparently they could hear my laughing all the way down.

For thousands of years, Anticosti Island was the territory of the indigenous peoples who lived on the mainland and used it as a hunting ground. The Innu called it 'Notiskuan,' translated as "where bears are hunted" and the Mi'kmaq called it Natigosteg, meaning "forward land."

Dad told me amongst other things, that the French explorer Jacques Cartier sailed along its shore in the summer of 1534. He provided the first written description and named it Isle l'Assomption, because he discovered it on the feast day of the Assumption of Mary.

In 1612 Samuel De Champlain spelled it Antiscoti, and from 1632 on it was called Anticosti and France had officially incorporated the island into its colonial empire.

The first settlers arrived in 1680 when King Louis XIV gave Louis Jolliet the Seigneury of the Mingan Archipelago and Anticosti Island as compensation for exploring the Mississippi and Hudson Bay. Equal to one-quarter the size of Belgium, Anticosti thus became the largest island in the world to ever be privately owned. Louis Jolliet erected a fort on Anticosti and in the spring of 1681 settled there with his wife, four children and six servants.

His fort was captured and occupied during the winter of 1690 by some of the Massachusetts troops of William Phips during their retreat after an unsuccessful attempt to capture Quebec City. After Jolliet's death in 1700, the island was divided among his three sons and the Jolliet family retained ownership until 1763 when the island became part of the British Empire under the terms of the Treaty of Paris that ended the Seven Years' War. That same year the island was annexed to Newfoundland until 1774 when it was returned to Lower Canada and annexed again to Newfoundland from 1809 to 1825.

The island became permanently part of Quebec at the Canadian Confederation in 1867. During these years the island property changed hands several times, its owners generally using it to harvest timber but otherwise no real development took place. For example, the French Canadian Gabriel-

Elzéar Taschereau owned it among other seigneuries and made money from them.

In 1895 a French chocolate manufacturer Henri Menier purchased the island for $125,000, he also leased the shore fisheries rights. Menier named the Island's Vauréal falls 70m (230ft) after the town of Vauréal in France where he owned a home. He constructed the entire village of Port Menier, built a cannery for packing fish and lobsters and attempted to develop its resources of lumber, peat and minerals. Many of the original houses stand today. He also converted the island into a personal game preserve and introduced numerous animal species not indigenous to the island for this purpose, including a herd of 220 white-tailed deer. The deer thrived and today the population exceeds 160,000 while the islands moose population is about 1,000. The bears which used to feed on berries to bulk up on for the winter, had lived on the island until the introduction of the deer, but have disappeared since the deer ate all the berries.

Henri Menier died in 1913 and his brother Gaston became the owner of Anticosti Island. He used and maintained it for a time but eventually decided it was not an economically viable operation and sold it to the Wayagamack Pulp and Paper Company in 1926 for $6,000,000.For the next five decades, the island is used almost exclusively by logging companies which invested nothing in environmental or heritage protection. The villages at English Bay and Fox Bay were abandoned.

In 1937, the year after I was born, my father Edmund James was employed by The Consolidated Paper Company as the office manager. In that same year, the government of Nazi Germany, led at the time by Adolf Hitler, tried unsuccessfully to purchase the island. Canadian Prime Minister William Lyon Mackenzie King became involved, and forbade the Nazi plan.

"Anticosti"

Edmund James Gallagher

Let us remember these upon this day

Who cometed no brightness through the sky?

Of history; who learned to play and cry,

Love and to marry, in their anonymous way;

Whom, being born in darkness, found a light?

Private and personal, by which they ran

Their unrecorded marathons of man

Unlocked by fame or fortune through the night

For in remembering in oblivion,

That populated country in the shade,

We learn how legends of the great are made,

Why every man is named Hyperion,

Titan of light, transmitter of its seed,

And sire of each prophet's burning creed.

Harold Zlotnick.

Appendix

FOREWARD

The first draft of this manuscript was submitted to Eileen, Sister James Marie S.S.A, of St Ann's Academy, Victoria, and B.C. Her enthusiasm about my Anticosti story was so encouraging that I added some recollections about our family. As a matter of fact, instead of my story being only of my trip around the Island, it has become in addition, an explanation of how we happened to be there, what the place looked like, what sort of people lived there and so on. Some of the story is now Eileen's, because when she asked me to write a piece about the scarlet fever, I could find no way to improve on her memo, and have included it just as she wrote it.

Having procured a map of Anticosti from Ottawa, I am astonished at the great number of place names shown. Some of the names, I feel sure, have never been heard on Anticosti.

E.J.G.

CHAPTER ONE

ANTICOSTI FAMILY

In September 1936, our youngest of 8 children, John, had been born just five months earlier; I made a trip in a motor boat around the Coast of Anticosti Island, stopping for brief visits at the homes of most of the game wardens and light keepers. I thought that upon my return I might prepare an account of the voyage for the entertainment of the family. I made some brief notes en route.

As it turned out I did not even start upon the task for many years. Some of my notes had already been lost when my sister Nora, undertook to try and type those that remained. It was an impossible task because they were indecipherable to anyone but me. I had forgotten their existence until Nora returned them to me.

Upon glancing through them, many of the events came back to memory so vividly that I determined to carry out my original intention and set them down in a readable form. That gave me a chance to add some descriptions of the island as I knew it, and any other items of interest concerning our lives on the island that occurred to me as I wrote. I thought it time to write of why we were there.

It was in 1928 that Flora and I left Montreal with four children to live on that island. The move was brought about by circumstances and our method of dealing with them. It happened that Michael was just 17 months old when Terry was born, and Joe came along fourteen months after Terry, with Eileen following nineteen months later. In just under five years of marriage we found ourselves with three small sons and a little smiling daughter. Whatever thoughts other young couples may have on the subject, we certainly did not embark upon our marriage career with any thoughts of founding a family or discuss the possibility either. Be that as it may our first air castles were planned for ourselves alone.

Almost immediately we learned that marriage brings responsibilities, and that ideas must be rearranged to meet the exigencies of the moment. The so-called formative years of children are at the same time formative ones for the parents. We have come to realize that all years are formative for persons of any age.

Baby years are preparatory for childhood; youth comes from childhood and are the years of adventure and achievement. After which follows the downhill run: a swiftly changing scene through middle age to advanced years, while the mind develops a habit of looking backwards and forwards, reliving the past and regretting the errors, exploring the future, at first with alarm, but with a growing interest and wonder.

Flora and I looked back on the years of struggle and worry as the happy years, the years of accomplishment. We recall and probably wearied our listeners with hearing the tales of our children when they were small, and what one or the other said or did.

A few of these stories must be recounted here because they are so much a part of our story that they must be used as a background.

Michael and Terry had a companion to play with before Joe was old enough."Dixie" was a clear-cut figment of their imaginations. They used him a lot as a messenger, and had to call him frequently by telephone to give him directions. The telephone receiver was a closed little fist pressed to an ear; the other fist was the transmitter.

The telephone was always located in a corner so that they could lean against a wall to talk. What "Dixie ever said to annoy them we never found out, but sometimes they would become exasperated with him because he was so slow to understand, and they would have to articulate very slowly and distinctly. In the "Dixie" days Terry was very punctual about his morning nap. If he was not put into his cot, he slept nevertheless: he simply rolled over on the floor and dozed off at eleven o'clock, leaving Michael and "Dixie" to play on together until he woke up again.

After "Dixie" they inaugurated an era of trains of upended chairs. In the chair train each chair had to have an operator, and without moving an inch, eyes shining and muscles tense, they would speed along leaning over for the curves, shouting for their mother to watch out, and Flora, entering into the spirit of the game would jump aside, hand on heart, just in time to escape being run down.

Sometimes she would delay the train by picking a protesting engineer out of his cab to kiss him, or to send him to the bathroom. That train was in operation in their home for many years, new engineers and engineer-esses replacing the super-annuated ones.

Early in Joe's career he decided against submitting to the constraint of a po-chair; and mastered the art of using his enamel vessel without superstructure, navigating from room to room in pursuit of any kind of diversion. A regular port of call was the bottom of the kitchen cupboard where he would stop long enough to toss all the pans and things onto the floor.

Eileen was gradually accepted by the boys as an equal in many of their games, and their superior in some, but she also had her place as a little girl to fill; and the boys and I soon came to realize that we had two women in the family to deal with.

With such a family it soon became clear that the C.N.R. Land and Townsite Department was not going to pay me sufficient money to live on during the years I would need it most whatever it had to offer for the distant future. Accordingly after a period of praying for guidance, planning, and numerous interviews, I found myself talking to L.A. Brooks C.A. in the office of The Anticosti Corporation. He offered me a job as 'Paymaster' which I accepted.

In July 1928 I left Montreal. Flora followed with our family and furniture in August. As usual we counted heavily on the help of mother and Joe. Mother said afterwards that when she returned to Montreal after saying good-bye to Flora and the children at Quebec, she had the feeling of having pushed them in the river. But I was waiting for them, and when we got ourselves settled into the apartment house we knew that everything was going to be alright. Michael was six and a half then and Terry four. For them the baby pages had already been turned.

One immediate advantage of the change was the solving of the space problem. The children could get out playing. No more worry about sidewalk tricycle riding. Another advantage that Flora and I both appreciated was that although my office was a busy place with first claim on my time, the fact that it was so close to our home made a great difference in our family life.

It was no longer a question of my leaving home in the morning before the boys were dressed and returning after they were in bed and asleep. I was now able to see them every day in daylight, instead of just on Sundays, and I could share the pleasure and the responsibility of their companionship. We had breakfast together and they were often out to play before I left the house. We had dinner at mid-day with time out to talk things over; and in the evening I could lend a hand with baths and haircuts, lessons, stories and prayers.

From the time Michael started school at the French convent under the devoted Sisters of Charity, until we left the Island ten years later, the "locomotive chant" was a familiar chorus in our home, and in the summer time when the school windows were open, the strange spelling lessons would resound around the village square; lo co lo co loco m-o m-o locomo t-i-t-i-ve locomotive.

Our children were divided into two more or less distinct generations before Anticosti and during; that is the first group of four were born B.A. and the second group of four who came along in the succeeding ten years during Anticosti of. D.A.

We never talk of the baby days of the B.A. group, without including my sister Margaret, the children's Mungie, in our thoughts. She was a one-in-a-million sister. Margaret was with Flora a great deal of the time through the months before

Michael's birth, always a tiny tower of comfort and strength. It was Michael who changed her name to Mungie, from his earliest vocabulary, which name her husband Bill took a fancy to later on, and has called her by ever since.

Through the Terry and Joe crisis, (pregnancies) she was never very far away with her practical advice or kind help, and when Eileen came into the world, Flora and Margaret were alone together, waiting for her.

The two and a half years difference in age between Eileen and Patty separated the two groups of children. Michal being the oldest was the leader of group one, which little by little absorbed the second group led by Patty, for some activities.

Michael had a wonderful happy nature and a gift for organizing games for any number of players of all ages, and for allotting to each a specific role. If his leadership was challenged at times by Terry or Joe they usually settled their differences themselves without appealing to the parental court.

We had very little of that to do and as a matter of fact, it is surprising how much we never found out about what they were up to, even when they were very small; for instance Terry told us only recently about how he and Michael used to have endurance contests in the corners of their room trying to go to sleep standing up. They were never able to decide a winner of that one.

As the older ones graduated from chair, trains, rocking horses, toy trucks and aero planes, and went on to scooters and coaster wagons, skis, toboggans and snow shoes, air-rifles and fishing poles, sling-shots and kites, boats, bicycles and cameras, there was always someone coming along less sophisticated and content with the simpler playthings.

In the evenings we played table tennis, ring-toss, darts, monopoly, rich uncle or some other game. If they bested mother or dad, they had good reason to swagger because we never made it easy for them to win; but there came a day when we were well pleased to win a game once in a while.

We tried to make Christmas a time to remember and we have reason to believe we succeeded. It was our hope that in preparing them for life, they would not suffer in later years by our separation from city schools and associations, and in this also we feel that what they missed in one way was compensated for in another.

A family laugh that has come with us down the years, started when my description of a thrilling circus event I had seen in my youth was challenged by Michael; "Did anybody *else* besides you see that?"

CHAPTER TWO

ELLIS BAY

Sometime about 1925 or 1926 several paper companies had financed a six million dollar deal to acquire Anticosti Island from the Menier family who had owned it since 1896. The transaction turned out badly for nearly everyone concerned except the Meniers.

Anticosti Island has repeatedly resisted exploitation with all of its cantankerous nature. By 1936 all that company had to show for ten years of operation was dismal failure, typified by the half mile or more of dilapidated wharf with its single uneven railway track; extending from the shore to the rim of the reef, where it forked to thrust two arms into deep water, forming the "cargo wharf" and the "loading wharf".

Part of the space between the two wharves had been in busier times a concentration pond for pulpwood.

In 1936 two immense steel loading towers still reached skywards, their cross-arms sagging dejectedly, having been rigid in that position for years. The spectacular jack ladders and conveyors, which had operated as part of the loading system, had long since been dismantled and removed; having been an eyesore, and offensive to holiday seeking guests.

It was both exhilarating and depressing to compare the present doldrums with the busy days gone by; and to remember the sounds and sights that had been part of the wharf activity from early spring until late fall.

There had been the screech of the saws as they slashed through the twelve foot logs fed to them by the pike-pole men at the jack ladders, cutting them down to four foot lengths which were tossed onto the conveyors. There was the dull bumpy bump sound of the wood as it rolled along, until tumbling into the pond with a splash.

When it was down it was taken up again. We were told this was an engineering error but it looked efficient nevertheless. A giant bucket suspended from the cross arm of a loading tower, would be plunged into the wood-filled pond to sink of its own weight and entrap a dripping cord of wood at each dive. It would then bound with its prey into the air like a live thing, and clatter along its overhead track to the other side of the wharf, to drop its burden with a reverberating thud into the waiting barge.

The memory of all the noise and fuss was like distant sweet music to our 1936 depression conscious minds. Even in the old days the actual noise was comforting, because we heard it all night even in our sleep, and knew that our jobs were still safe. Any cessation was so startling that a sudden quiet would awaken us

Boats large and small were constantly arriving and departing, the dredges of the Foundation Company and the Company schooners Cherisy and Joliet. The company tugs, Hullman and George M.McKee, and passenger and freight steamers, S/S Fleurus, Sable I, Gaspesia and New Northland.

 Then there were Water Transport Company pulpwood barges, called the "water boats" because of their names: Surewater, Swiftwater, Deepwater, yachts of wealthy Canadians and Americans, the Molson's and the Mellons to name one of each; the Lady Grey, with on one occasion Mr. Michaud and party, and again Mr. Duranleau and family, at times an icebreaker; and occasionally even a warship from England or France.

There were familiar faces and strange ones, bosses, visitors, Catholic and Protestant clergymen, seamen, woodsmen, auditors, clerks, wives, children, horses, pigs, cattle, activity, blessed work, pay cheques, excitement, jollity, hope, tragedy, in a word, humanity at work. The majority of the woodsmen were French Canadian but there were stolid Europeans as well. They were mostly hard working Polish men.

......and now in 1936 there was hardly anyone in sight. Many, perhaps most, of those cheerful hardworking men had gone to swell the ranks of the unemployed in Quebec City, Montreal, and many of the smaller towns along the St. Lawrence. The wharf was now our promenade, our boardwalk, and above all our gateway to freedom; but we never used it as such because we feared freedom with its spectre of unemployment more than we feared exile.

Nevertheless, the fact of the "open door" made a difference in our lives that was incalculable. We hurried to the "bout du quai" for all occasions of meeting and greeting and parting, the seasons' arrivals and departures.

We watched the wharf being almost submerged by the high tides of early autumn that crept in stealthily under the hypnotic power of the harvest moon, until the Bay was full to overflowing and all the empty gasoline drums afloat. At other times we watched facing up to the wild gales of late autumn. The accumulated wear and tear of years of unrepaired buffetings had brought about its present state of dilapidation.

Half a mile across the Bay due west from the end of the wharf was the inner shore of the peninsula (without a name) that forms Ellis Bay. We often ferried ourselves over there in a small boat in the summer time for a picnic and a swim; and in winter we crossed on skis or snowshoes just for the fun of it. We liked to get over the headland as early as possible in the spring and out on the ice for miles to the edge of the water just to reassure ourselves that the river was still flowing under the ice.

One summer was almost ruined because a great dead sperm whale lay decaying on the shore. A number of these huge mammalian submariners were thrown up on Anticosti's shores that summer, and later we read a news item informing us that it was a worldwide phenomenon. Sperm whales had been found dead at the same time on the shores of Australia and New Zealand, and the scientific explanation was that they had died of pneumonia caused by some shifting of the Gulf Stream.

The point of the peninsula a mile or more to the left, say west south west, was known to us as Cap Henri but is called by its English name on the map. It is so well protected by reef that ships coming from the west had to sail a couple of miles below the village before turning in to come up by the channel; and even after rounding the buoy great care had to be taken to keep the range signals in line.

At night, particularly, the possibility of mistaking a light of the Villa for one of the range lights was a hazard indeed. The open end of the badly bent horseshoe that was the Bay was the door by which the southeast wind blew in from the Gulf of St. Lawrence; and fifty miles almost due south, which would be taking a sight from the village over Cap Henri, was Fox River the nearest point to us on the Gaspe coast.

Westward were the inner reaches of the Bay, and the Villa Menier, built on the very spot where a hundred years earlier the home of Louis Oliver Gamache had stood. Louis himself, whose story is told by Monseigneur Guay in 'Lettres d'Anticosti,' is buried on a hill overlooking the Bay, and a pointed wooden slab marked the spot in our day. Legend had it that he was buried kneeling up. His wife also is supposed to have been buried there but the grave was not marked.

Michael, Terry and Joe used to explore every nook and cranny of the Bay in their boat in search of driftwood. Often they would return home dog tired and hungry as wolves, but immensely proud, their boat almost sinking under their load. Often they had several logs partly water logged, in tow. The salt was not good for our stove, but it was cheaper to fit new linings in the fall than to buy firewood all summer.

Chapter Three

Our Port Menier

At the shore end of the wharf a branch line of the railway turned right to seek shelter under the roof of the unloading platform beside the sheet metal covered warehouse. The main line pushed inland to the old logging camps.

Another tin-roofed building with about fifteen steps leading up to it could be seen from where I was standing. This was the general store operated by the Company where the employees exchanged their wages for food, clothing and a thousand other necessities including beer, wine and hard liquor. Charles Boudoul, one of Menier's men from France, and a French army veteran, was the 'god' of supply and demand. That 'god' presided over the council of buyers in the Montreal purchasing department. We thought of him as a most unfriendly 'god' because inevitably we paid more for everything than the prices quoted in the newspapers, even after adding handling charges from Montreal to Anticosti. Also, we called him a most uncivil 'god,' and we did not always stop there.

Camille Lejeune, second generation of the name native to Anticosti was store manager and an excellent one. Camille and his large family were neighbours of ours and one of his little girls, Camilla, was a bosom friend of our Patty. They learned to walk at the same time, and spent the first few years of their lives playing together in the grass or the snow, and always holding hands.

Eastwards along the shore from the warehouse, a row of identical red houses lined up as though for inspection, facing the sea along Cap Blanc which stared across the Bay at Cap Henri. All the Menier houses except his own interesting Villa were painted a box-car red.

Near the store and partly visible from the wharf was the little church, unique in many ways, but significant of prevailing conditions in the fact that the cure was on the company's payroll, and the pew rents of the faithful became revenue for the corporation . The little church had never looked like a church until Madame Pierre Casgrain, a personality in her own right since then, twitted Messrs. Faure and Ritchie into promising to build a steeple on it, which promise was duly honoured.

There must have been an interesting conversation in the comptroller's office the day that unbending person agreed to initial the work order. I have often wondered if M. Faure used authority, cajolery or bribery. At the rear of the church was a house for the priest. In our day, Anticosti was a Eudist Mission. A succession of devoted priests ministered to the spiritual needs of the almost completely Catholic population.

In miniature, the work of the mission might be said to exemplify the role of Catholic priests the world over. As readers, wise leaders, thinking men, but particularly as detached observers, they must often have felt the urge to lash out against 'man's inhumanity to man; (although during the depression there was probably more humanity evident at Anticosti than elsewhere); but due to Church discipline and their own training in wisdom, not one indiscreet observation was ever uttered to my knowledge.

As the first Apostles took their instructions from Peter, so did they. Far from fomenting unrest their quiet serenity had the opposite effect, except when there was some restlessness among the congregation at Mass on Sundays when Father Hesry attempted a few words in English for the benefit of the Gallagher's. As Apostles they preached above all the love of God, and demanded in His name decency, morality, dignity and echoing the words of the Master in His Sermon on the Mount they counseled patience in suffering.

In their austere and lonely lives they practiced the virtues they preached. To me it was a lesson in humility to have them call at the office for the curé's pay envelope. I never got used to having them sign for it. Father Hesry often came during the regular evening periods when the men and boys were being paid; and although all of them without exception would touch their caps respectfully and make a passage for him, he would smilingly motion to them to go ahead of him, and he would await his turn.The mission included the entire Island, and at least once a year they visited heir scattered parishioners, to celebrate Mass at the pavilions and lighthouses, to baptize, hear confessions, give Holy Communion, and comfort the sore oppressed. At times no doubt, they found a faith going dim after a long time without the Sacraments, and had to blow on the spark to set it alight again, and leave renewed instructions for obtaining the Grace of God to keep it going until his next visit.

Almost in line with the wharf stood the grey administration building-two stories', wooden construction, and beside it the little grey radio shack with the high mast towering above it. Between there and the church an old cannon that had been recovered from Baie Ste Claire was mounted. It was said to be from one of Phipps '. It could have been. Some of them came to grief there.

There was a large village square with a white flag pole in the center, and facing the square on the far side were more red buildings of various shapes and sizes. The two largest were the convent and the hotel. The most important to me was the eight–room house in between, with the high fence around it-my handiwork-(the fence that is) where Flora was a prisoner of our eight children. Danny, Margaret and John were born in that house. Patty was born in September 1928, the first baby of English speaking parents to be born on the Island, in the long house that perched on the high ground on the west side of St. George's Creek, where we dwelt during our first year In Port Menier.

This staff house, which we called by the higher sounding name of apartment house, was a frame construction, two stories high, built on a concrete foundation, with central heating, composition shingles outside and gyproc inside finish, with six upper and lower flats. It faced the bay and the northwest wind, and an old round, rusty disused eyesore of a chimney, maybe one hundred feet high, loose riveted and creaking, with a ladder up the outside that clanged in the wind. It had been a slash burner in Menier's time.

How the boys loved the open air and the prospect that unfolded before them as they raced up and down the long balcony and started making the acquaintances of the neighborhood.

The road leading westwards from the village crossed the creek bridge just below the waterwheel. Here on this bridge we stood each year to watch the spring festival of the sea-gulls which was celebrated by the birds when the freshet tumbled down over the dam. Crying in their seemingly joyous excitement they would settle on the racing water for a thrilling ride down to the bay, and then hurry back by air to the starting point where they would hover as they peered impatiently downwards in search of surface space.

 Over the bridge the road passes the power house and the apartments on its right, a freight shed and the old slash burner on its left, then on in a semi-circle around the bay to the Villa. On its way it passed four other more pretentious red houses, built by Menier for his key men, one of which we occupied during our last year on the Island; and the company-built house, pale yellow in colour, occupied in turn by all the Island Managers except C.R. Townsend who preferred the biggest and finest of the Menier houses, known before his time as Captain Pelletier's house. Captain Pelletier had been a high ranking personage during the Menier regime, but in the company organization he was merely sitting out a contract at a high salary and enjoying the situation.

Tancred Girard, another of Menier's men who stayed on with the company in a working capacity, was a large, grizzled, weather-beaten, handsome man with a rare smile. By his honesty, industry and integrity, he set an example of devotion to duty that was never appreciated by any of the high command except Mr. Faure. His skill in handling men, his knowledge of boat-building, from the cruising of the bush in search of "knees" to the final launching, were used unsparingly by the company but his rewards were meager.

The Girard's had one daughter who was married to Lorenzo Cyr, a dispirited fellow. Lorenzo did not have much of a job-a fellow had to take what was offered to him or get out-so he and his wife and numerous children lived in Girard's house, and it was Tancrede who paid most of the bills.

Tancrede's chief aide was old Eugene Chevalier Sr. who was stooped and grizzled, and as wise as he was sleepy looking. When he talked he mumbled, as if he didn't much care if anybody listened, but I learned that the effort to understand him was well worthwhile.

In Menier's time Eugene Sr. had had his place on the Island executive, but now after the change of ownership and times of depression, he was just one of those old reliable people who, for a pittance more than the lowest paid man on the payroll would uncomplainingly and efficiently act as timekeeper, shop runner or foreman of any kind of work gang.

He was never sick yet all but one of a large family of children had died of tuberculosis. The one surviving son, Eugene Jr., was the best machinist on the Island. Howard Watt flew Eugene Jr. and Dr. Whissell to Quebec when a piece of rust fell from the inside of a boiler where Eugene was working and cut his eye-ball almost in two. They saved the eye, but before the old doctor in Quebec learned that the accident had happened at Anticosti, he gave Whissell quite a dressing down for delaying too long in getting his patient into the hospital.

Eileen says I must write something about the house we lived in the last year of our stay on the Island. Before us it had been Dr. Martin's house for some years through the Menier era, and also with the corporation, but he lived in it rent free with all expenses paid. We did not. After Dr. Martin left, the house was vacant for years, and then when the hotel was closed as an economy measure, it was used as a boarding house. After that it was vacant again until it was offered to me as a token of something or other. I am still wondering about that, and how I could have been so foolish. It was big enough for our family to expand in, and everybody liked it. One big room at the top of the house was used as a photography room by Michael and Terry. It had a large conservatory where Flora had some nice ferns, and used to sit with her sewing and watch the children playing around the steps, or the boys out in their boat. It had a large sitting room with a fireplace for logs and it had a large furnace, with a very large door.

Patty fell down the steps one day, broke a milk bottle on the way down, and cut her leg badly. Eileen says in her notes:

"Do you remember the big doll she got for being good while the doctor scraped the bone, no anesthetic, no freezing or luxury of any kind?"

No my dear little girl, I do not remember any such thing. Patty received better and more skillful attention from Dr. Whissell on that occasion than she could have got at St. Mary's hospital in Montreal. He opened the cut wide to examine it carefully for bits of glass, and when he was satisfied it was clean, he put clips on to close it, and it healed like

magic. I think the little girl that was watching with her big brown eyes, was feeling the pain more than Patty was.

A scene that Flora and I witnessed together comes to mind. It is of a lanky boy, one of the Lajeune's, chasing a little wild duck up and down in the water in front of Townsend's house. Perhaps a foot and a half of high tide covered the reef. Not a ripple disturbed its surface, except on the race-course where the duck swam, pursued by the galloping boy, both of them dripping red with sunset water. Up and down they went in

hundred yard dashes, the boy winning each heat, but losing the race; because each time he overtook his quarry and stooped over for the grab, the duck would submerge and come up behind him, going full speed ahead in the opposite direction. We were afraid the duck would start laughing and get caught, but he did not. The boy tired first and stood still in the water, a picture of weary defeat, the most beautiful coloured comic in our memories.

CHAPTER FOUR

Port Menier Environs

The road turned right at Lajeune's corner, but topped with clean gravel now as it crept discreetly around the Villa grounds and stopped at each entrance. The road came to the end of that clean gravel and continued on its own dirt road as it resumed its own way westward. The dirt road continued on through the bush for nine miles to Baie Ste. Claire and West Point.

The road then branched off first to Rentilly Farm, where it turned right and ran a couple of miles into Lac Plantin where the aeroplane was based, and where the big trout lay under the mooring raft.

Another way of reaching this lake was by walking up creek Plantin. Flora and I sometimes put on our rubber boots and went for a walk up the creek when we felt the need for a change of scenery, but we seldom fished and never went the full distance to the lake. It was the boys' favourite trout stream, and they always returned with a nice catch of fish, frying pan size.

The creek's twisting course was a pleasant walk unless the black flies chose to attack. The boys had more than once reached the wooden dam where the lake overflowed into the creek, but had always returned by the same route.

The shore of the lake was marshy, and the ground so very soft that some called it quick-sand. Perhaps it was. I know that on one occasion I sank in it faster than was pleasant. I had agreed to accompany the boys-Michael, Terry and Joe, up the creek to the dam, and then to continue around the shore of the lake to the road. It was a beautifully fine Sunday and we got started after early Mass. I had invited Graham for dinner at six o'clock so Flora had a busy day ahead of her. I promised to be home in good time, but the boys fished, and took pictures, and we dallied over our lunch.

We were a little behind schedule when we arrived at the dam, but we really started to lose time as we splashed our way around the marshy lakeshore. We got pretty tired too, particularly Joe, who was always such a courageous and self-contained little fellow that we sometimes let him do more than he should before remembering he was younger than Michael and Terry. So he rode on my back and we splashed along slowly until suddenly I stepped into a pocket of this very soft ooze, and went a-sprawling. Joe and I were both proud of the fact that he kept his seat on my back and rode me like a rhino until I succeeded in getting perpendicular again. We were not awfully late for dinner because when Graham arrived and learned from Flora what our plans were, he drove to the lake by the rode, and met us. We planned to go again and walk all the way home but we never did.

The second cut-off from the main road branched left and slipped downhill through the woods to the seashore, a pleasant spot known as Anse-aux-Fraises, Strawberry Cove, as it is known in English. It was a good place for a picnic or a swim in the surf, but not a good place for anyone who disliked cold water. The children loved to pick berries there, and there was sand to play in where a gentle surf pounded. The main road continued on to West-Point where Horatio Malouin lived at the lighthouse with his family of about fifteen children and was responsible for all the fog horn mechanism. We visited West Point occasionally. Sometimes we went by car but not often. There were only a few cars on the island, four was the highest number I have known at one time, so we went by car only if invited.

But if we wanted to go to West Point, or Baie Ste. Claire or Lac Lac Plantin, or Strawberry for a drive or a family picnic. I could always get a horse, or a team of horses if I so wished, from Albert McComick, my friend at the farm. If I wanted to take only Flora, I could have a buggy, or in winter a single-seater sleigh. If I wished to take the entire family and any other picnic-minded friends who cared to go along with us, Albert would place at my disposal a team of horses and the big 'brake'.

I fell in love with this ancient vehicle the first time I saw it and I don't think anyone else of our era, ever used it but me. It was a very sturdy hack with a permanent roof, and side-curtains to let down and button in place if it rained. It had two side seats facing each other where about six persons could sit on each side, if some of them were small and a seat for the driver where three more could sit comfortably, and that makes fifteen.

With picnic baskets and thermos bottles for the older children and grown-adults, bottles of milk and a supply of dry things for the babies, a kettle and a frying pan, and an assortment of dishes; and feed for the horses, we sometimes spent from daylight until after dark away from home rumbling along the road. Flora singing, and the kids joining in; counting deer, sometimes over a hundred of the beautiful creatures between Port Menier and Baie Ste. Claire; keeping a lookout for reindeer, rabbits, foxes and all manner of wild things. We stopped to eat when we were hungry, Flora preparing the feast with lots of willing help, and I getting the fire going, finding water and feeding the horses.

After the feast, when the scraps were packed and the refuse burned, we would amuse ourselves playing tag, playing ball, wrestling, racing, fishing exploring. On one such outing we took mother to see the trees on the headland at West Point so buffeted by the wind that they could not grow upright, but became shrunken and gnarled and twisted, their tops only a few feet from the ground, forming an evergreen mat that a man could walk on.

At Baie Ste Claire, Menier had built his original settlement, and some of his predecessors had also lived there.

In the little cemetery there was the grave of a Stockwell baby boy who had been drowned in a bath. Here at Baie Ste. Claire we took mother to visit a favourite place where a great ledge of overhanging rock a thousand or a million years old, had toppled over, no one knows when. It stood up on its edge on the shore where the history of its forming lay exposed for those who could read it, like the open pages of a book. Here we could find in the rocks traces of petrified branches and twigs; and on one such page Anderson had discovered the vertebrae of a bird or fish. In our time the village had been abandoned as a settlement. It was almost a deserted village, but not quite. Most of the houses were vacant but there were still two or three families living in the ghost town.

One of the townspeople, an old man with a beard like Father Time, called himself the Postmaster. He was James Duguay, the older brother of Placide of South West Point, and Joseph, the Postmaster at Port Menier. He lived there with his middle-aged daughter, and kept a little store where he sold a few odds and ends to fishermen from the north shore that came ashore there to dry their cod-fish.

Also, he may have had the official appointment of Postmaster. If so, the only mail he would have to handle would be his own and that of Andre James, an enterprising member of the strange little community.

James, pronounced 'Jam', was a veteran of the French army who had fought through World War 1. He was dying of consumption, but he stayed on his feet coughing constantly and smoking cigarettes without ceasing, a chain smoker. Regularly, he laid in for resale a stock of good liquors, liqueurs, and wines of all descriptions which he procured from a schooner bootlegging out of the French Islands of St. Pierre and Miquelon. Andre was a widower, and he lived there with his ailing children, apparently all suffering from the dread disease: a son, several daughters and a baby. He cached his wares in the cellars of the empty houses around him.

We had a distressing experience once, which we never wanted to repeat, and have never forgotten. We were out for a drive with Fred Anderson in his car, and thought we would buy a bottle of whisky. We sat in the shabby room dimly lighted by a smoky coal-oil lamp, surrounded by the painfully polite anaemic daughters while James went out to one of his cellars. The saddest-looking of the girls was holding in her arms the sick little baby who fretted weakly in piteous whimpers. Presently James reappeared out of the shadows with our 26oz. bottle of Johnny Walker Black, for which we paid him two dollars, and departed. That baby died a few days later. We took Patty out of school for a year, when one of those girls passed the teaching examinations and was appointed to the convent school in Port Menier.

This was all the road there was from Port Menier westwards. Possibly less than thirty miles for the round trip and go everywhere a car could go. Another road followed Creek St. Georges northwards for a short distance, then crossed it above the dam, and skirted Lac. St. Georges. It came out at the farm in about fifteen minutes walking time. There, Albert MvCormick toiled - the perennial optimist: "Next year the potatoes will be better, or we had too much seaweed in the soil this year, that is why the centers are all rotten are all rotten; or I told that man from Ottawa that I could grow potatoes if I could be left alone." or, "The vet. from Montreal says a half of the herd have T.B. and have to be destroyed. I told the boss that would happen if the company could not afford enough fence to keep the elk from grazing with the cows." It was true that the elk had T.B. because Townsend shot one that had got dangerous and when it reached the market the doctor condemned the meat as unfit for sale.

A short distance beyond the farm was the fox ranch where successive managers tried unsuccessfully to operate a clean-smelling industry. The main idea behind the founding of a fox ranch was to raise a pure strain of silver blacks that could be released a few at a time in the hope of gradually improving the wild strain that inhabited the island. Some of these had been imported by Menier, but some must have found their way over on the ice from the north shore. Lemoine tells about a shipwrecked crew having eaten fox meat for two hundred years earlier.

As a result of the ranching, a slight improvement in the quality of the fur may have been noted, but it was hardly recognizable. Most of the pampered foxes released did not know what to do for a living when they found themselves alone in the wild, and so fell an easy prey to the rigours of winter, or poachers, or perhaps even to their jealous mongrel cousins. Some were "pelted" at the ranch and the furs sent to the auction sales in Montreal, along with those collected from the trappers, but on the whole it was a costly experiment.

That road to the farm was a bleak walk on a stormy day. The boys used to go there to discuss farming and fox ranching and kindred subjects, and to ride the horses. One blustery Sunday afternoon, when they stayed too long, Flora at first became uneasy and then panicky, and raced out in search of them. In her haste, she neglected to put her ski pants on, and her skirts being not much protection, she was painfully frost-bitten by the time she returned, with the remorseful and solicitous boys.

On another occasion the boys were driving along that road in the dusk of the evening to return a horse and buggy they had borrowed, when they had a most unusual experience. Two six foot wire high fences ran along each side of the road. A deer came racing across the field towards them from the right and it saw the first fence on the one side of the road in time to clear it in a beautiful leap, but not noticing the second fence on the other side it ran full speed into it, and recoiled as if from a catapult falling in the road directly at their horse's feet. The horse reared in fright and the deer, instantly realizing what had happened, leapt up again and cleared the fence in a second remarkable leap leaving a terrified horse and three startled boys staring after him. The boys arrived home still breathless, their eyes shining with excitement as they all tried to tell the story at once.

The road through the bush eastwards from the village was known as Canard Road. Canard was just a collection of old log huts falling to ruin, about nine miles up the coast. The old logging road passed the village dump about a mile away, so we rarely went that way except on skis when unsightly places were covered with a blanket of snow.

Chapter Five

People We Knew

Still looking shoreward from the end of the wharf, and imagining what cannot be seen because the view is obstructed by the warehouse, store, or church; one turns the hotel corner and passes the tennis courts to face the largest red building of all- The Clubhouse- erected as such by Menier. Here through the long stormy winters when news of the outside world reached us only by radio, unless, weather permitting, mail planes arrived at intervals of about three weeks, the population of Port Menier would gather to spend their evening.

Badminton, billiards and pool, target shooting, were in progress most evening within the club, and a tournament of one sport or the other was usually under way. There was a good dance floor and a piano, so it was not much of a problem to get a dance started anytime. In addition, a hockey schedule was played on an outdoor rink on Saturday and Sunday afternoons, which kept interest at a high pitch. You chose your favourite sport either as a player or spectator and having done so, it was hard to remain neutral, because likes and dislikes had a very personal quality.

Instead of listening to hockey over the radio, we stood in the cold to watch each game to the bitter end, holding our ears and stomping our feet. What was happening to the N.H.L. was of secondary importance. Organized activity at the club slackened as winter followed winter but our interest did not. All that was needed was the opportunity. In the old days when the steam plant was operating there was an abundance of electric power and constant interest in the club; but later when the economic doldrums set in it was a different matter.

A water wheel was installed in the creek, and when it was functioning there was no problem even in the depression days, but the wheel was motionless during the winter. Another phase of the depression was that the cost of running the diesel engine to supply comfort or frivolity, or even fire-wood for the purpose of recreation was vetoed by the High Command. Oil lamps therefore became the vogue in our houses, and gasoline lamps in the office and store. Badminton could not be played very successfully by lamplight, but Coleman or

Aladdin lamps well placed could be used for billiards or pool.

There were occasions however when the diesel engine had to be kept running for legitimate purposes such as pumping water, or supplying power to the machine shop, or for the lights on the wharf, and at such times the lights in the club were turned on.

The names of our fellow exiles from 1928 onwards through 1938 come to mind. Each succeeding winter meant changes in personnel. There were more "good-byes" than "hellos". The year 1928-29 was the third such hibernation for some of the staff, the second for others. The Islanders, those who knew no other home than Anticosti and who had been taken over by the company from Menier as a moral responsibility, (although I would venture a guess that acceptance of the responsibility was not voluntary) kept or were kept very much to themselves. For the outside staff, houses were hard to come by but the Montreal office did not engage anyone for whom they were not prepared to find some kind of accommodation.

Consequently, hotel rates were not designed for profit making and many single men and several married couples were able to do very well out of it. The apartment house answered the problem for those with children, and for a few married couples who liked their own space rather than a motel, even though a more expensive way of living. In the apartment house there was a constant battle with bugs, the most horrid experience perhaps we ever had. Not the least annoying thing about it was that some of our neighbours denied ever seeing them in their apartments, even though the partitions were only gyproc. I kept a rubber syringe and a bottle of turpentine handy. Bob Murdock and his wife Nan who were our next door neighbours, were our allies in the siege. As a matter of fact Mrs. Murdock warned us with a disgusted look, immediately when we moved in, what it was like. We were on our guard from the first day.

The Murdocks came from Scotland. Bob was office manager-in his mid-fifties-heavy set and jovial and Nan "the best wife in the world" was about his age and a bit on the heavy side. Bob had worked in Montréal with Anglin-Norcross for years, a construction clerk. The Murdocks loved to entertain and play Bridge, and the boys from the hotel did not need coaxing to go there. Mrs. Murdock didn't resent us moving in beside her with our big family on the other side of a thin wall. Instead, she was very nice about it, and loved the children rather rather too much. She fed them so many cookies that Flora had to make rules. She used to say in her broad Scotch "they wake up in the morning chirruping like wee birds."

Bob was an ardent fisherman. Time stood still for him as he stood on the bank of the creek casting for trout. He had been in the butter and egg business in Northern Ireland and he liked my name because he had some Gallagher friends in Donegal. He used to tell tall tales of his boxing days in Scotland, and when he had "had a few" it was a good thing to watch out for a sudden left jab that he might use to illustrate his talk. He also had a story about how long-years I believe, that he had kept an egg fresh on his desk in Ireland by changing its position every few days so that the yolk should never touch the shell. We spent many evenings in their apartment and they in ours. We played Conversational bridge, planned our bug strategy- discussed the neighbours in whispers, and when we were in their house listened to their nice records. My favourites were " Danny Deever,", "The Road to Mandalay", "No Wonder The Waves are Wild". There were few radios on the island that winter. Murdocks left the next year.

On the other side of us was Percy Harrison, woods foreman and above us in a row the Kelly's, The Mchenry's, the Frappiers. We blamed the Frappiers for the bugs because they said they never saw any. The McHenry's we did not know very well. Pat Kelly, whose correct name was Peter but Bill to his wife Freda, came from New Brunswick and Freda was from England. Pat was a veteran of that last great cavalry charge at Caix Valley in 1918. Their son Peter and the Harrison's boy Bobby, were pals of Michael and Terry. When our Patty was born Mrs. Kelly was very kind to Flora. She was very kind at all times, but more of a reader than an efficient housekeeper. She laughed at herself about it and was very good-natured when anyone else did. She invited the children and me up to a meal when Flora was in bed being looked after by Mrs. Mercier. Mrs. Murdock, afraid that the children would not get enough nourishment at the Kelly's, filled them up with "good Scotch broth" on the quiet so that they could not do justice to Mrs. Kelly's banquet. Bob Murdock and Mrs. Kelly are both dead now, God rest them. Mrs. Murdock went back to Scotland and by now she may have joined Bob.

Emery was chief electrician. He was from Maine-called himself a maniac. His wife was French from St. Hyacinth, QC.

M. Henri Valiquette was Island Manager then. He had replaced McLaren who there before our time, and he in turn was followed by Townsend in 1931 and Graham in 1936. Valiquette's era was in the days before entertainment accounts went out of fashion. Parties at Valiquette's house were fun. Madame Valiquette could instantly arouse enthusiasm in lethargic guests by perambulating from room to room holding aloft a bottle of Scotch, or rye or gin, and chanting . " Qui m'aime me suit". Nearly everyone followed. By profession, Valiquette was a Civil Engineer, and since he knew nothing about logging his job was a sinecure. In the years since he left Anticosti, in his own field he has established a reputation as an efficient administrator as Town Manager in Three Rivers.

Charles Gosselin, the Woods Manager, was a Forestry Engineer, and Valiquette's right hand man; but he helped more with the enjoyment of life than solving problems. Gosselin never seemed to have got over the wonder of having mastered the slide rule. He talked with it always in his hand, and seemed to be able to use it for every purpose, even searching for the right word.

The Woods Foremen under Gosselin, Brolin, Harrison, Lindahl, and later Lindgren and Frolisch, were a sterling lot, and the real bosses and planners of woods operations. Percy Harrison was the only Canadian. The others were Swedes. All had wives except Brolin, and all except Harrison lived at the hotel, or in the bush.

My boss, Fred Anderson, was Chief Accountant-a bachelor who lived in the hotel until it closed up, and then in a bachelor apartment alone. He had been a woods accountant with the Laurentide Corporation at Grand'Mere and he had an enormous amount of confidence in his own ability; but only skepticism about ever being able to find it in others. His main job was to bring order out of chaos in an office which had been notoriously unsatisfactory. Gosselin's conviction that bush accountants were the lowest form of life, supported by Valiquette's low opinion of accountants in general, presented an accounting problem that no known diplomatic approach could solve.

Anderson was picked by Brooks for the job. He was silent and unapproachable. It was only after a long time that I discovered a sense of frosty humor lurking behind that cold exterior. After that he and I got along very well together until he left the Island in the spring of 1935. Anderson was always a success as an organizer of club activities, particularly badminton tournaments. Each succeeding year he would devise some new and original plan which he would keep strictly top secret until tournament time. One year his surprise package contained an ample supply of Gestetner made booklets of badminton regulations, with a special section for local court rules.

Another year he installed an efficient badminton scoring gadget made of colored wooden blocks strung on a wire, nine blocks yellow and one red. The red blocks had their numbers painted on them in white. The billiard idea applied to badminton.

In the depression days when he moved into his bachelor home, he bought a Delco light system and had cheerful electric lights when no one else had. He was a good host, and often shared his light. The batteries needed a lot of attention and he did all the work in his basement workshop.

Flora and Anderson and I sometimes went skiing on Saturday afternoons, and one day we got lost in the bush and created quite a sensation. We had left the children alone at home. Michael and Terry were always trustworthy, and the smaller ones too for that matter, but we fully expected to be home before dark which would be lots of time for supper.

However, it was long after dark when we struggled home through a snow storm to a frightened family and an excited village. Anderson led us home. The fire bell was ringing to summon men for a search party, which was being organized and about ready to leave. I still think we might not have been so completely lost and have made so many wrong turns in the bush had I been well; but the scarlet fever got hold of m that day and I was out of circulation for a long time afterwards. Lucky for me we had Dr. Whissell on the Island then. We had a great turnover in doctors, and the outstanding one of all on all counts was George Whissell. He saw me through the scarlet fever and the quinsy that followed it. He fixed the terrible cut on Patty's leg, and he pulled Flora through a bout of pneumonia. Joe was the first to introduce the scarlet fever into our house, the night of the incident of the deer on the farm road, and he was a very sick boy with it. Then one after the other all the children had it.

When it seemed that we were finally through it, I borrowed some money and persuaded Flora to set out for England with Danny and Margaret who were babies. Michael, Terry, Joe, Eileen, Patty and I said we could look after ourselves. Flora got to Montréal, embarked on the Duchess of York, disembarked at Québec, and sent me a message to say that she was not going through with it, and was on her way home again. We were overjoyed to have her back, and that bout with scarlet fever was my peculiar way of celebrating, which I topped off with a round of scarlet fever arthritis. I do not think I would have lived through it if Flora had not been there.

Eileen, who had become the editor of this story while she was a nun in Victoria B.C. said; "I think you are the only one who can tell about scarlet fever, or mother. She was the nurse. However I remember a couple of things. One is the big long-sleeved white apron which mother wore when she tended a patient. Another is that I picked skin off my fingers with a pin in order to expedite the business of "peeling." I wonder how mother could tell it was not genuine. I wish I could get in more about mother. There is an epistle taken from The Book of Wisdom that is read at Masses for women saints, who were considered great, like St. Ann and St.

Elizabeth of Hungary. It begins, "Who shall find a valiant woman?" I think of mother whenever I read it."

Eileen, I can tell you another little story about your mother that will make you laugh. Do you remember the Frasers? The two Fraser brothers, Ross and Bryant (known to everyone as 'Happy') lived with their mother, the widow of an Ontario small town doctor. Happy was a correspondence school civil engineer who had come down in the early company days, and had won the attention and trust of operating department heads by his ability, his enormous capacity for work, and eagerness to accept responsibility plus a remarkable self-confidence. He had sent for his mother and older brother Ross, who was a clerk in the warehouse office under Renaud. The contrast between the brothers was striking. Ross's chief interest in life was bible study. Like 'Happy' he possessed unlimited confidence in himself, but unlike his younger brother, was more interested in bible discussions and attempting to convince his friends that their religious beliefs were faulty, than in applying himself to work, as did 'Happy'. The righteous non-Catholic logic has such a dreadful chill on it!! The Frasers were a little tiresome. The mother, a very large woman called on Flora, and while rocking vigorously in one of our wickerwork chairs tossed herself over backwards. Fortunately she did not go right over, but stayed propped up against the wall until extricated. Flora laughed a little in her confusion and seriously upset the older woman's dignity. Their friendship never did warm up. Flora was always too busy for small-talk friendships anyway.

Howard Watt was not a permanent Anticosti resident, except for summer flying, contracts with the company when he would come with his wife Flo, and camp near his plane at Lac Plantin. Nevertheless, his unexpected comings and goings through the years must be allotted an honoured place in my Anticosti Ledger.

He was, and is, an airman. His flying days started in the first war and ever since then, up to the present time, without too much of the kind of learning that comes from books, he has kept planes in the air when they should be up; and he has made it a habit to set them down on skis, or floats, or wheels, right side up, under conditions that sometimes would be impossible, except that in his flying experience he has never used that word carelessly.

Through our Anticosti days he used to drop in from the skies at unexpected times and in any season. It was always a pleasure to welcome him. When he took off from Anticosti the day after Christmas 1937, Michael was in the plane with him, on his way to his first job, working for Howard, and being initiated into the marvels of aeroplanes.

During the second World War, a grandfather by then, his air sense, cool daring and good judgement enabled him to apply what he had learned from coaxing those early crates into obedience along the St. Lawrence; knowledge that had been added to as newer and better planes came into his possession. He applied this exceptional know-how to the business of flying Mitchells, Boston's, and Baltimore's across the oceans. These he would park in England or Africa as surely as a few years earlier he had whirred down to a smooth landing in a blinding snow storm. Through the war we welcomed him from time to time, and even now, we still look forward to his less frequent surprise visits and his exciting, well-told tales of distant people and faraway places, or business deals closer to home, with a carefully calculated risk to give it a zip. A Shrewd, independent, efficient, cheerful Howard-smooth landings always is our wish for you.

CHAPTER SIX

MORE ABOUT PEOPLE

Dr. Martin and his chic little wife, both from Paris, had come to the Island in Menier's day and remained for a time with the company after the sale. When he decided to leave the company, several more attractive offers failed to induce him to change his mind. He brought Daniel Martin Gallagher into the world, and he fixed Joe's broken leg. Only recently we have learned that Joe grew to manhood thinking that Flora and I had set it ourselves. We often spoke of the Martin's during the war, when Paris was in such a sorry plight, but we have never heard how they fared. Arthur Renaud, married and father of a large family was also a Menier man. He was from Québec. His wife was an Island girl, a Richard.

Arthur had been very badly gassed in the 1914-1918 war, and had volunteered to undergo some tests to aid research, but is health had been worsened, if anything, by the result. He had been well treated in a pension way, but never knew what it was to be entirely well. He quickly wearied of the Island under the new regime, and returned to his native Québec City where he became and still is a Pratte & Cote man.

We moved into the Renaud's house when they left. I always think of Arthur Renaud as one of those special people you consider it a privilege to have known.

The office was the better for having Dunc Wathen in it. Dunc was from Moncton, about twenty-seven years old, interested in his work, and everything he did was well done. Single, heart-whole and fancy free, he was a great favourite with the ladies particularly the unmarried ones. When typhoid struck that winter of 1928-1929, he had a bad time of it. Most of us boiled our drinking water and took all the precautions that were recommended. Dunc looked on such precautions as foolishness, and insisted on drinking the clear cold water in the club. He used to challenge fate by exclaiming: "Boiled water? Not for Dunc! Let's have a drink of typhoid water". He had a miserable time in the hospital and barely escaped with his life. After he left Anticosti, Irving the great in Saint John knew a good man when he saw one. Dunc has done exceptionally well for himself.

Bill Moir also was a young member of the office staff and a great favourite with the married ladies. He was tall, blond and very handsome, but completely unaware of it, Bill cared not at all for romance. He was a man's man, although only a nineteen year old man, and liked badminton and bridge, serious conversation and spirited debate.

Alberic Julien was from Québec City. He was a payroll man, and the distribution of the time sheet charges to all of the 1928-1929 operation costs was a job to keep a man working early and late. Alberic played a good game of hockey, was dependable at badminton and billiards, bridge and chess, and in addition was a connoisseur and mixer of strange and wonderful drinks with a "sleeper" of alcohol hidden in every fancy name. He had a nice little side line selling Philco radios, and kept a horse and sleigh for his week-end outings.

Maurice Valois, a great little guy from Montréal, fixed us up with our first radio by setting up a loud speaker in our living room, a most decorative ship with sails, attached by means of a telephone wire to the radio in his room in the hotel. Maurice was a fiery little fellow and once in a game of badminton he got in such a rage at himself for muffing a shot that he broke his racquet over his knee. On another occasion he committed mayhem on his billiard cue.

Eric Hall about my own age, thirty-two then, single, from England, worked in the office. A big powerful chap Eric was and an expert billiard player. He could break a hundred regularly, on a bet. Thinking about Eric reminds me of the McGill Travelling Library. He looked after it for a while and kept the records. Of all the contributions to the general good of the nation that McGill is credited with, this service seems to me to belong at the very top. Those lists of books for old and young to pore over and order from were a blessing indeed. The boxes each contained forty books and they cost four dollars a month for each box, paid for out of club funds. Isolation has no meaning any place where the McGill Travelling Library can reach.

Bill Routledge, also from England, and Charlie Perkins from Barbados, contested Eric Hall's billiard supremacy stoutly. Both were very good players but not, I believe, as well as Eric. Bill does not agree with this, so it will never be settled. Charlie certainly cannot dispute it because he used to muff shots before spectators that were easy for him in practice games.

Eric and Bill played as if they were the last two men left alive in the world and the outcome of their play would decide the last survivor. Their politeness to each other during such a match was something to see.

The billiard players had some exciting competition the winter Cope crash-landed his aeroplane on the ice of the bay, with a ski hanging loose after a bumpy take-off, and spent the rest of the winter packing his wounded bird for shipment by steamer–freight, and playing billiards. He was English too and knew all the rules.

Although Bill Routledge came from England he had made a trip through western Canada with a harvest crew, before coming to Anticosti. This trip and his varied experiences in England which included a walk from Carlisle to London, as well as years of old country railroading, added a lot of interesting material to the general conversation. At Anticosti he was an electrician and Emory's right arm, consequently he had a lot to do with the power house and all of the intricate electrical installations on the loading wharf.

Down in Barbados they know a lot about model ships. Charlie Perkins built a most beautiful model sailing yacht for our boys. How they loved It.!

Zatezalo, unmarried, from Vienna, a veterinarian among many other things and master of most Europe an languages, stood up to Leger Noel the policeman, in a boozing tournament. Noel was quite a finished performer, but Zatezalo had enthusiasm. He did not win but came p smiling through his gore at the end of a grueling contest.

Then there was Fitzpatrick, the saddler from Newfoundland, large and ruddy with a friendly grin who had a blood curdling oath which he would rip out with great gusto when he missed a ringer pitching horseshoes. The horrible swear words were; Sac-re-men-t, taber-nac or colis. Well, that's how it sounded to my Anglophone ear.

Reggie Arseneault, single, from the Magdalen Islands was the badminton champion. No one ever beat him as far as I know. Bob Hunt could probably make him exert himself more than anyone else, but I do not think he ever beat him. They used to say that Reggie got lots of practice in timing at the hotel where he worked. At washing-up time, Lacey the cook, and some other joker used to toss hot plates at him and Reggie was so constituted that he could not let them pass but remained fixed in his place and caught all they threw,

Lacey and his wife were English and had two little girl's not yet teen age. In addition to being cook at the hotel, Lacey was also chef at the Villa when the Montréal hierarchy where in residence, which made him a well of information for the gossips.

What Lacey did not know about anything or anybody was just not worth knowing. He was an authority on etiquette and dress, and could be very engaging discussing such nice distinctions as the difference between "dress" handkerchiefs" and work "handkerchiefs". Above all, the Laceys were bridge addicts and when their own turn came to have a party, the village was a buzz of anticipation beforehand, and of appreciation afterwards.

Herbie Peters of Québec QC (outside Anticosti) lived as a bachelor in the hotel because his family preferred off the Island Québec. Herbie's grandfather had built the Villa for Menier.

When I think of Bud Muirhead, I always remember him standing in the midst of a group of high-spirited gamblers, on the hotel verandah, in a high wind, shaking dice and waving a roll of bills in a general good-humored challenge. On the floor were the bets, many ten dollar bills showing, each man holding his own money down with his foot. It was not a paying game for Bud that day. He had to go and find his boss, one Elsliger, a loading contractor, to get another advance his pay.

Another memory of the hotel that I shall always cherish, although uncertain of the year, is an evening spent with several other veterans of World War I in the company of Canon Scott, who was a guest there. I had heard of this beloved padre, and had seen him once in France at the Canadian Corps Sports at Tinques in 1918, but never talked to him.

He gave one of his famous lectures in the hotel for anybody who wanted to hear him, and afterwards he invited any veterans present to come to his room for a chat. "Sit here on the bed with me Trench Mortar" he said to me, "it isn't lousy." He told us tales of men he knew, of experiences he had had, both funny and tragic, of searching amongst the dead for his son, of a flight over the front lines in a crate that bumped over the ground so crazily before it could be coaxed to take off, that he felt like the Irishman in the sedan chair without any seat in it, who remarked to his friend: "Faith and if it wasn't for the honor and glory of it, I'd rather walk." He autographed for us some of his verses printed on small cards, and I think the most human of all, and he most enlightening as an insight into the work of an army chaplain after the fighting stops, was the one that says:

Bill White came home

And found his wife

And in her arms a baby

At first he said: "It isn't mine",

And then he said: "It may be."

And so they lived for many years

A credit to their station,

And all because he gave to things

A kind interpretation.

He said as we were leaving, that he had enjoyed the evening as much as we, but that was just his way of talking, because it was no novelty for him to be the center of a group of veterans.

CHAPTER SEVEN

Weather Report

The weather must of course be mentioned casually here and there throughout my story, but I believe I should devote a special chapter to the winds of Anticosti. One must get used to them to live there. Looking back on it now it seems to me that it never was never really calm. It was not always on the rampage of course, but you always had to be ready for it even if you were just going for a walk.

I had better begin with the wild storms of winter and follow through to the quieter seasons. I am open minded regarding the theory that Canadian winters are becoming milder, even allowing for the fact that a snow drift, like most other things, looks a lot bigger to a small boy than it does to his father. Nevertheless there was little indication during our years in Anticosti that any serious attempt was being made towards lessening the severity of the storms.

They were heralded by the appearance of ominous mountain of clouds that swiftly formed themselves into a dark blanket. Then fitful gusts of wind started and stopped again like a sprinter testing his getaway. At this point the storm signals were usually hoisted on the mast near the office, as the weather reports came in.

In our day this hoisting of the signals was the duty of Joseph Duguay, the Postmaster. Soon heavy wet sticky snow would commence falling steadily hour after hour. On the way to work it might have been up to our ankles. Coming home again, depending how late we worked, it would be up to our knees, our thighs, and our waist. After a day or two the wind would veer to the northwest. Storm signals would be changed, the cone being turned upside down with a square blanket below it, to announce that the wind would be of "gale" proportions. The thermometer would drop to zero, sometimes to five or ten Fahrenheit below. It seldom went much below that.

A few freaky very still mornings it may have gone to twenty five or thirty below but zero weather with that wind was about as cold as anyone could wish it even for boasting. After all, we were not searching for gold in the arctic but just bringing up our family of children five hundred miles down the St. Lawrence River from Montréal. Usually there would be a few hours of ominous lull while the north-west wind was getting set to blow, and then as if from a standing start it came at us across the Bay in a mile a minute rush, and kept on blowing for three days without stopping. In places it blew away all the snow and left the ground bare, and in other places piled the snow in drifts twenty, thirty, forty feet high. Near the apartment house we actually stepped over the electric light and telephone wires.

Joe broke his leg jumping for a snow bank out of a window in Emory's house. He was only a little fellow following Michael and Terry and Bobby Emory on an escapade while Mrs. Emory was out shopping. He missed the snow bank and landed on the frozen ground.

High up over the storm the sun might be shining and the sky blue, but on the ground one would never guess it. We apartment dwellers never used our front doors during a storm. As a matter of fact we sealed up our front doors and windows so well that we hated to break the seals. I whittled a stick with which to plug the key hole where the snow was drifting in, and in the morning a snow ball as big as a baseball, had formed around the stick.

Opening the front door meant that we might have a lot of trouble shutting it again, and in the meantime the snow would sift all over the house, with the sitting room carpet puffed up into waves. In our second house, two weeks after Margaret's arrival and on the very day that Flora was to get up for the first time. I came downstairs on a stormy morning to find that the porch door had been left open a crack as I could see through the glass of the inside door, and that the porch was filling up with snow. Thoughtlessly I opened the door to see what could be done, and I saw very quickly. In a twinkling all the snow in the porch had been puffed into the front hall, allowing the porch door to open wide. We were completely exposed because I was unable to close either door. I hurried, got my cap and gloves and raced out the back way. The kitchen door closed after me with a bang that shook the house. I grabbed a shovel from the shed and started around for the front but I did not race. I got down on my hands and knees and crawled inch by inch, dragging the shovel as I went.

My immediate task was to get the porch door closed which I eventually did. Inside the house was a shambles. Our sitting room was to the left of the front door and the dining room to the right. Every chair and every piece of furniture in both rooms had a mound of snow on it. All the way up the stairs was a sloppy mess and there was snow on the children's beds. It was only later that I learned that at the time I chose to open my front door the wind had been blowing at ninety miles an hour. Flora did not go back to bed. She stayed up and directed salvage operations.

Through March and April those north winds still carried the chill of icebergs from Labrador or from the wastes of Hudson Bay; even though by then they were softening perceptibly week after week, and helping the sun wear down the great snow drifts. By the middle of April they would have broken the ice bridge across the Gulf of St. Lawrence to Gaspe. What a sight that was. After months of obstinately refusing to move, the ice under the steady pressure of wind and tide would disappear from sight as quietly as clouds cleared from the sky and the wonderful grey and white water would laugh and sing and dance in its new found freedom.

In May during the daytime, the snow banks would honeycomb rapidly under the warmth of the sun and disappear at the touch of the drying wind; although at night the melting away would be arrested and you still knew that same wind had crossed over the ice and snow of the North Country before blowing in to visit us.

Notwithstanding the fierce storms, I very much want to avoid giving the impression that we looked upon our life at Anticosti as a great hardship. It was never such a thing. We had more fun twelve months in the year, a happier home life, and less worry than people in our circumstances in the city will ever know. Our trouble was that the depression kept us chained to those circumstances when we wanted to advance; but Anticosti Island offered us some generous compensation. More of this later as it does not belong in a weather report.

The months of June to October were delightful. Not like a tropical isle to be sure, but then we are not tropical birds. Only those who have known a heat wave in Montréal-those oppressive humid days that follow airless wakeful nights when a bed sheet is too much covering will appreciate the thought of a cool lovely climate where, if the temperature got above 70f and there was no wind, it would be considered "pretty hot weather-phew pas fret m'sieu;" and if it passed 75f some of the old timers would be tempted to change from their heavy woolen underwear into something lighter. The only reason such extreme measures were never taken, to my knowledge, was the certainty that such heat could not last. We practically lived outdoors all summer because unless it was storming or blowing too violently we never closed a door or a window but just let the sea breeze whistle in through the screens. We had to cover up with blankets at night of course. In all our time down there, no one ever slept without bed-clothes, on purpose.

Needless to say since the welfare of the children was the reason for having moved from Montréal, this wonderful fresh air and freedom and the children's exuberant reaction to it, was our greatest happiness. They never needed coaxing to be active. On the contrary, it seems to me that the most overworked words in my vocabulary were- Hey, cut that out." It was not all play for them either. They had fun, everything they ever did had laughter in it, but out of their fun would appear as if by magic, stacks of firewood in the shed which had been bought as four foot logs of black spruce and birch, six to twelve inches thick.

I do not think I ever asked one of them to touch a saw. As a matter of fact I am sure I withheld permission a long time before giving in. I was rather afraid of saws and axes especially for little boys.

I knocked myself out cold when my axe caught in the clothes line and knocked me on the head. "It's a good thing you weren't using a double bitted axe" said the doctor "It would have cut through to your neck." Cutting and piling firewood was not their only occupation, far from it. To them this was just an incident in a busy day. There was usually a cash consideration to be discussed, but there was no need to haggle because their demands always began, "Spose you could spare---?" And if I could spare, (Which was not always) they would go into a huddle amongst themselves to apportion the scandalously low wage. Eileen was sometimes in on this split, having piled her share of wood and entered her claim. When Danny was big enough, by their standards, he was taken on as Joe's helper and sometimes came in for a cut. Berry picking was a popular activity. Flora usually organized these excursions and often joined them. Their take would be wild strawberries, raspberries and blueberries. The golf course, where just about no golf was played at all, was the favorite place for picking wild flowers or berries or having picnics close to home. It was also the place for flying kites, playing ball, or just running. "Can we go out—we just feel runny?"

The fastest travelling bad news to reach us on the wind was the unmistakable odor of forest fires. After a dry summer it was inevitable that the sky should be overcast and the color of the sun changed to an odd shade of pink, while the acrid smell of smoke hung in the air. Usually the fires were far distant from Anticosti. Sometimes the smoke would blow up from the Maritimes or over from the Gaspe, and sometimes down from Northern Quebec or eastward from Ontario; but always the warning for us in the message was the same, "this could happen anywhere." There was never any anxiety about the people of Anticosti being careless. They appreciated the danger and took every precaution. Once, and only once, during our stay a bush fire really got going not far from Port Menier.

I was away off the Island at the time and had Joe with me. Flora was alone with the other seven. There were quite a few men around to fight the fire. There was a heavy pall of smoke, and the crackling of green spruce burning could be heard distinctly. Their eyes were red and watering, and the air at times was hard to breathe. Smoke blackened men kept warning Flora to be prepared to leave the house at a moment's notice if the fire came any closer; and this state of alarm and uncertainty kept up for several days.

Fortunately the wind shifted, and the rains came. Joe and I came home a few days after it was over and felt like deserters sneaking back to camp. The shortening days of autumn and the prospect of approaching winter were perhaps the most depressing of all the year. About the time the last boat was ready to leave, Flora would get uneasy about things that might happen during the winter. Nearly every fall or winter something would happen to somebody. Several persons died during the typhoid epidemic and a shed near the locomotive shop had to be used for a morgue until spring. There was the constant fear of tuberculosis because there was so much of it all around. Fabien Noel's little girl was drowned. The Apestiguy boy was shot. The Bourque boys were lost through the ice. Paul Anglehart froze to death. When I promised Flora that I would not let anything dreadful happen to us my confidence was largely based in the

knowledge that she would not let things happen.

CHAPTER EIGHT

UNDER WAY

The time was three fifteen in the afternoon of September twenty-second 1936, when I went aboard the "Courcelette". The launch was commanded by Francis Boudreau, a native of the Island, a short saturnine man in his fifties, French Canadian by name and language but bearing in his features and manner the unmistakable stamp of antiquity which suggests that some of his forebears may have been watching from the shore as Jacques Cartier sailed up the St. Lawrence the first time.

His son Ovila, a younger edition of the father, acted as mate, engineer and crew. The passengers were: a sick boy going home to his parents at Riviere La Loutre; a young man on his way to spend the winter as assistant to the Light-keeper at South West Point, and I, the company's office man stationed at Port Menier since 1928, and starting my first "around the Island" tour. The purpose of my trip was to take stock of all corporation property of a 'vanishing' nature wherever it could be found. I was an assistant to a new broom. I was also burdened with the task of delivering to nearly all of the game-wardens, letters containing the unwelcome news that their wages were to be reduced October first. The only wardens not to receive such a letter were those whose wages were already at a demoralizing minimum; and as these were living in the hope of better times, my duty was not a pleasant one. The boat was dirty, grease spattered and untidy, as motor boats usually are, but an office man, and particularly an employee of a big corporation with a stern disciplinarian in the office of comptroller, is sometimes glad to leave routine and exactitude behind him for a few days whatever the conditions.

After a careful glance around, Francis motioned to Ovila who gave a deft twirl to the fly wheel and the expedition got under way. A small group waved from the wharf and we all waved back. Years of experience had made Francis familiar with the hazards of the Anticosti coast, but familiarity had bred respect and not contempt. On his ship he assumed full authority and while navigating never relaxed his vigilance. Also, with full knowledge of the reef and its dangers, once clear of the channel and beyond the point which formed the Bay, he kept his boat well out to sea. The

Honourable C.C. (Chubby) Power in speaking in the House of Parliament at Ottawa about the dredging of this channel had caused a slight ripple of amusement by calling it "ain't it costly".

I had planned to stop at Riviere Canard and Petite Riviere, but was over-ruled by the Captain who stated several reasons to prove that it would be folly to do so. It would soon be getting dark. There was so little equipment of any nature left at either place that it was not worth stopping to look at. The camp in question could be reached more easily by driving down from Port Menier.It was going to blow very hard soon, and already the sea was rougher than he liked it and he would rather not stop before Becscie. His case was flawless, and I readily agreed, because I knew that his real reason for haste was his anxiety to deliver his little sick grandson to the parents at Riviere La Loutre.

I sat on a coil of rope and gave myself up to reverie, enjoying beyond words the freedom from my desk and the fresh air. I tried to piece together in my mind a stirring description of the Anticosti coastline. The words bleak, rock-strewn, reef guarded, windswept and desolate, kept intruding themselves so persistently that others more flattering were crowded out. I found also that a continuous repetition of these words fairly describe all that there was to see with the physical eye; yet I felt I was not being fair because the sum of all these words made a hopelessly depressing total, and to me such was not the case. Notwithstanding its harsh treatment of many, its centuries of cruelties recorded and unrecorded, this sullen Island of the frowning coastline and the raging storms had given me a measure of security and hope for which I was grateful.

For over eight years it had allowed me to provide adequately, if not abundantly, for Flora and our children who with the arrival of John the previous April, now numbered eight. Michael and Terry were New Brunswickers, Joe and Eileen Montrealers; while Patty, Danny, Margaret and John were, as previously noted, all Anticostians.

After several years of national economic depression I had come to realize that my course had been set in 1928 by an all-seeing God in answer to some fervent prayer. Yet I was not satisfied. Although as I say, I was grateful, I was also like the Island itself, sullen and cantankerous. I am afraid my employers were my dearest enemies.

My difficulty then in describing the Island lay in the fact that my feelings towards it were in such conflict. I needed to express bitter hatred and at the same time acknowledge humble love, intense gratitude and such burning animosity that even now as I write this, twenty years later- it is 1948 now-I can still feel a faint resentment at the galling caution that kept me chained to that isolated Island for so long—over ten years—exchanging the best years of my life for the bare necessities. Only now, with the wisdom that comes with the passing years, I know that the caution was the Grace of God imposing on me, at least in relation to my family, the qualities of trustworthiness and reliability.

My reward has been very great. I enjoy the esteem of my wife and children without ever having been a money-maker. My precious Flora never became a drudge. She has radiated love and happiness upon her family year in and year out. She would make her children happy even while scolding them, and now, although children no longer, they still laugh delightedly as they recall some of her pungent thrusts. Since first she came from England to marry me, she has accomplished the impossible day by day, year after year, with no apparent effort. In her sweet voice she has sung her way through every difficulty with a gay song most of the time, a ribald one sometimes, a sad one very, very, seldom.

The children learned to join in those songs, before they could talk, and they do it still for that matter-all but Michael. It is chiefly from their letters, but in many other ways as well that I knew that the material successes I coveted, recognition in the company and decent pay for me, lighter duties for Flora, good schools and golden opportunities for our children, would not have been best for any of us.

We are a hard working lot, and the smooth roads are not for us. Strangely enough, this conviction only came to me recently, as I mused over a letter I was writing to the Imperial War Graves Commission about Michael's grave at Imphal in India. Michael once told us about flying over Anticosti Island on one of his many flights out of Ancienne Lorette, and of pointing out to his pilot the house we lived in for so long. That very house might well have been the theme for the following poem written by Stewart Evans and published in Country Life, London, which also appeared in the Montréal Gazette:

House of his boyhood day

Do you still know his step?

His warm young hand upon your sturdy
oak?

Do you remember how he moved and
spoke?

Another world ago?

Hopes of his brief score years,

Are you engraven yet

Upon those lichened walls or writ more
light

In the salt winds that whispered through the
night.

To empty rooms that wait?

Swiftly he laid life down, its riches all
unspent.

High noon was not for him, yet who's to say

That he has lacked the glory of the day

Who saw the morning break.

CHAPTER NINE

Becscie,Ste.Marie, La Loutre

We arrived at Becscie at about five-thirty. It was here that I spent a night with Karl Lindahl in 1929 when he was experimenting with a log-bundling machine designed to obviate the necessity of coastal towing, a ruinously expensive operation. Maurice Valois had been there too, "cache clerk" as we termed it. Maurice had turned out early in the morning before I embarked for my return journey to Port Menier and from a favourite pool had produced six beautiful salmon, averaging about eighteen pounds, for me to take home. His lure was a piece of hay wire with a slip knot in the end.

A mythical tale has come down through the years, founded upon circumstantial evidence and horrid imagination that a case of cannibalism once occurred at Riviere Becscie among the survivors of a shipwreck. It could have been, of course, but a story about Becscie that I like much better was told to me in 1928 by the cook of the logging camp, about his efforts to trap a bear that was making a nuisance of itself. He baited a barrel with chunks of pork and then drove a number of large sharp nails through the barrel from the outside, pointing inwards and downwards, hoping the bear would go head first for the meat, and get himself caught on the nails. The bear didn't want to play it that way. He upended the barrel and dumped the meat on the ground scoffing it at his leisure.

Logging operations had ceased in 1930. By 1936 the chief summer activity was providing luxurious salmon fishing opportunities for the wealthier citizens of the United States. High prices had discouraged Canadian anglers.

Antoine Lelievre, the resident warden, came out in his boat to greet us. A first rate-man, Antoine was. A tireless man, he was an intelligent guide, popular with the sportsmen, attentive, keen-eyed and pleasant. He was also one of the best trappers on the Island. It took him only a few minutes to transport us and his supplies ashore. He was then ready to accompany me on my snooping tour. Prying into company affairs which touch so closely upon a man's family life is an embarrassing business. Before I had finished, I quite appreciated Antoine's dismay when he learned that some article which he considered his own property had been listed as belonging to the company. Sometimes I hesitated to press a point, feeling that if I stuck too rigidly to the old list, without making allowance for error, I might find before my tour of the Island was completed that some careless clerk in prior years had absent-mindedly written "rocking-chair-kitchen-with game warden's wife attached".

There was a great quantity of logging equipment stored at Becscie, left over from busier times, so by the time I had finished listing it all, it was already growing dark, with everyone hungry, and the house and pavilion still to be checked. Antoine's wife Georgette, young, pretty, capable, and with a gallant spirit, had supper ready: canned salmon and boiled potatoes, good homemade bread and gooseberry jam with an orchestra by two year old Lucille. By the time I had finished my work, Francis had decided that we should sleep at Becscie and make an early start. I was more than willing. I had a chat with Flora by telephone with all the lines on the Island open, but we were used to that. Afterwards I listened as well as I could to the French conversation and joined in occasionally. The talk was all about fishing and the personalities who had visited the Island to fish. Such names as John Foster Dulles, the Pews, Jay Cooke, often were heard in the conversations of the Anticosti guides.

Francis was the first to yawn, and as I had been waiting just such a signal, I made my way to the pavilion where I had the most comfortable bed assigned to me. In two minutes I was sound asleep, and in what seemed like two minutes Francis was telling me it was five-thirty and time to get up.

I washed and shaved in cold water and was tempted to try a swim but lacked the fortitude. I went for a brisk walk in the cold air, and then sat down to an appetizing breakfast of eggs, toast and good coffee. We had a long row to the Courcellete but were on our way again at six-thirty. The sea was perfectly calm although Francis was sure it was the calm before the storm. Nevertheless I could imagine no more delightful situation for a man to be in, than sitting warmly clad, in an open boat on a cold fall morning, smoking a pipe, after a wonderful sleep and a good breakfast.

We went ashore at Riviere Ste. Marie at seven-thirty. This river can be a good salmon stream but is not a sure fire producer like La Loutre or Jupiter or even

Becscie. I delivered the letter but found, as was to be expected that the telephone had brought bad news. It seemed that Georgette Lelievre thought bad news travelling by motor boat was not fast enough. Jim Dresdell the nominal warden would not be concerned about it if he heard that his pay had been stopped altogether.

 Madame did all the worrying. Jim according to legend was rightful heir to the lands and fortunes of the great English family Draysdell. I do not know if there was such a family, but when I was at Ste. Marie, Jim was quite convinced that he was not made of common clay. He could not read or write, and he spoke only French; but only the fact that he had carelessly mislaid the papers necessary to prove his claim, keeps him from his inheritance, and if ever he has time to look for them in the drawer of his desk, the Draysdells in England will surely have to recognize him. With what bushels of malarkey that first Draysdell to reach these shores, must have overawed his little Micmac bride. Was he a soldier, sailor, explorer or trapper? Whatever he was he had firmly established the Draysdell's right of privilege for generations to come. Jim's Madame seemed to accept the fact that his hands were not meant for work. She looked after the river with the aid of her boys, and assumed all responsibility during the busy season. She cooked for the fishing parties, managed the younger children and instructed the older boys in their duties as guides, trappers, or the activity of the moment. She collected their pay, attended to the wedding details when they wished to get married, and went right on having beautiful-flaxen haired babies.

"Not Angles-but angels." She accepted the pay cut with businesslike common sense, as if she quite understood the workings of the executive mind, and appreciated the necessity for stern measures at Head Office. She decided immediately to bring a few children home from the convent in Port Menier to balance her budget. She turned her cupboards inside out for me to check her possessions and gave me a list of things she would need for next year, such as a large roasting pan and a replacement for a broken platter. She offered us all breakfast which we declined threw us into our boat and gave us a shove. I felt as though I had been through a washing machine and wringer, remarkable woman.

We left Ste. Marie at eight thirty. It was always a surprise to me how far we had to get away from shore to be in the deep water. A bleak wind was blowing and the sea was getting rough. Francis was right as always. Our stop-over at Riviere La Loutre was hurried. We delivered Joe Apestiguy's small son to him. As I expected, the news of the pay reduction had been received by telephone, but I could never be certain in advance, of the manner in which the news would be received. It got to be a guessing game in which I was right most of the time. Joe accepted the letter in hopeless resignation as he lived his life. Joe and his brother Vincent, the warden at Galiot, came from France, I believe, in the service of Menier, but both had been away from the Island during the war years as soldiers. One went with the French army and the other wore the kilt of the 85th Highlanders from Nova Scotia.

Joe's wife was the oldest of Francis Boudreau's several daughters, and together in this depression-ridden land, they were worthily bringing up a large family, but to judge by their habitual air of sadness, happiness seemed to have eluded them. Undoubtedly the Anticosti warden's lot was a hard one. They lived as wards of the owner company, of which fact they were constantly being reminded, and the inference was always present that if they knew of a better place to go, the sooner the better. Consequently their independence was forfeit, and the vision and hope and enterprise of the pioneer, non-existent. Nevertheless, most of them managed to retain the happy-go-lucky carelessness of the Quebecers whose trust is in God, the parish priest, and the political leaders of their own Province, in that order; and who have their large families in happy defiance of orthodox economic principles. Why Joe should have been weighed down by circumstances more than others I could not say, unless because a true French-Canadian must be born on the soil.

Whatever the reason, it seemed to me not only on that occasion but other times as well, that he and his wife had no defiance, no happiness, only submission of a most despairing kind. When sometimes prior to my visit one of his young sons, hunting with a shot gun had accidently shot his younger brother; and when the wounded lad, after days of waiting for a storm to subside, was brought by boat to Port Menier , only to die of gangrene poisoning, the despair in Joe's eyes deepened. I remember at the time trying to tell him how sorry I was but finding it impossible to speak, because of the utter misery in his face.

There was nothing lacking in the children. They were a bright, intelligent little group, perfectly happy and normal and well trained, with cheerful smiling faces. Joe himself was a popular and efficient guide, dependable at any work he undertook, but always silent. Madame was pleasant and neat and obviously a good mother. She had a reputation for being quietly efficient, and if La Loutre River was where she had to be, then there was nothing to be done about it.

CHAPTER TEN

A MEMORY OF JUPITER AND SOUTH WEST POINT

A high wind was blowing as we left La Loutre. The waves were high and as our boat plunged along we huddled in the cuddy and ate lunch, canned trout and boiled potatoes splashed by sea-water pouring through the roof.

Somewhere about half way between La Loutre and Jupiter, looking shoreward I was reminded of a time three years earlier when Townsend and I had slept one night on the sand. I had enjoyed every single moment of that trip. Charles R. Townsend, Island Manager then, dead these many years, had asked me to make the trip with him because he knew how much I would enjoy a change from the office. We had travelled to Jupiter on the M/V Joliet, an Island-built schooner with a powerful diesel engine. The Joliet like its builder Tancrede Girard, had served Menier well and was now doing the same thing for the company, it was starting its fall trip around the Island. The Jupiter is the aristocrat of Anticosti salmon streams. The warden's house at that time was at the "mouth." Fishing parties were never delayed there, but transferred painlessly by horse drawn barge to the swanky pavilion at "Twelve Mile." The strange river-craft was a heritage from Menier. It was known as Cleopatra's barge. I had heard all about these Jupiter camps many times but had never seen them. There were other less pretentious camps at 'Thirty Mile" and "Forty Mile." Once I read an account of fishing on the Jupiter River written and published by a member of a famous party many of whom have become more famous in the years that have passed since the time of their visit. Lewis W. Douglas has been President of McGill College and United States Ambassador to the court of St. James since then. Also since then he has lost the sight of an eye through a mishap while fishing in England. Mr. McCloy has had a tough assignment as civilian administrator of West Germany. According to Mr. McCloy's story which was accepted as true by his anything but gullible companions, and emphatically affirmed by Moreau the guide, he hooked a beaver one day above Thirty-Mile, using a trout rod, and after an exciting battle succeeded in beaching him, after which he let him go.

When Townsend and I were at Jupiter this same Rodrique Moreau was the warden. Townsend's intention was to examine the camp at Twelve Mile and to instruct Moreau in the matter of certain much needed repairs. We slept the first night at Moreau's house at the "Mouth." In the morning Townsend, Moreau, and I started up river, Moreau poling a canoe laden with provisions and sleeping bags. Townsend and I walked along the rocky bank together, exchanging war reminiscences, and discussing "The Dop Doctor" which he was reading at the time. The weather was cool, and perfect for walking, and we enjoyed the changing view as we followed the river upstream particularly the high sand banks which from a distance looked like crumbling castles. In the sand were sea shells so old that they could be rubbed to powder between the finger and thumb. The pools at "Three Mile" and "Six Mile" were hard for Townsend to pass without putting his salmon rod together but he resisted the impulse although promising himself to have camps built for the use of fishermen on their way upstream. Later the rain came down and the matter of just walking, crossing the river from time to time to find easier footing, required our full attention. It rained that day as if the Flood had started all over again. We were a very weary and bedraggled trio when we reached Twelve Mile Camp. Moreau wasted no time in starting a fire and soon the most delicious smells of bacon and coffee made us happy.

We wrapped ourselves in blankets and hung up our clothes to dry. Before we started our meal, Townsend uncorked a flask of scotch and we split it three ways.

The next day was bright and fine. We were up very early and Townsend, the inveterate fisherman, was out casting before breakfast. He took a salmon from the famous grey pool to start the day. His tour of inspection completed, and the necessary instructions having been issued to Moreau we returned downstream by canoe arriving at the "Mouth" in the late afternoon where we again enjoyed Moreau's cooking and Townsend's salmon.

Soon after we had finished eating we set out to walk to La Loutre, and had gone half the distance, a beautiful moonlit night with practically no wind when Townsend decided we had gone far enough. An old wound in his leg bothered him sometimes, and the drenching of the day before had not done it any good, so we opened our sleeping bags and slept comfortably on the beach. We had breakfast in the pavilion at

La Loutre and later walked up the river almost to its source carrying the Graflex camera turn and turnabout. The camera shots we got hardly justified the effort. On the return journey Townsend demonstrated his woods prowess by leading the way through the bush for a short cut, and coming out at the exact place he wanted to. Even Joe Apestiguy was impressed. It was a most delightful day spent in the best of company.

At the time of my trip around the Island in 1936, Charles Townsend was no longer Island Manager. Graham had taken his place. I saw him only once after he left the Island. We shook hands as we passed one day on Victoria Square in Montreal after I too, had left the Island for good, and then I never saw him again. Much later I was told that he joined the Forestry Corps and went overseas with the rank of Major. I was also told that he won his commission in the field in World War I which he had never mentioned to me. He did not return from WW II. Becoming ill overseas he was invalided home but died during the crossing and buried at sea.

On the 1936 tour, we passed Jupiter without stopping. The inventories are all at "Twelve Mile" and "Thirty Mile" mostly empty cans and salmon boxes, which were to be counted and reported upon by the warden. Canned goods used to be left in the camps until the bears took a fancy to canned fruit. They would remove the panels from the camp doors to gt at the latches, then once inside it was no trick at all for a smart bear to open up a can of fruit with his claws. Charley McCormick used to say they read the labels and had a preference for peaches.

The sea was so rough that we were all very wet and cold when we arrived at South West Point, but we received such a hearty welcome from Placide Duguay that I was ashamed. I had often met him when he visited Port Menier, and at times when he called at the office in a demanding mood, I am afraid I was not always entirely civil.

A hunchback with a kind smile Placide was the light keeper, a Federal government employee and only in a small way did he have business with the company. He trapped of course, and earned premium on the furs he turned in, and I also think he was on the payroll for operating a telephone switchboard. At any rate he turned out to be an embarrassingly hospitable host. He gave us a drink to warm us up, and then a cup of tea with rolls and jam. The prospect of an approaching gale prevented us from rounding the point and continuing on our way, which circumstance afforded the good Placide genuine pleasure.

After lunch I went for a walk to stretch my legs and to keep active while my clothes dried in the wind. The lighthouse, built in 1831 was undergoing repairs. All the windows were covered with sacking, a compressor was making a horrible noise and two of the most efficient workmen I ever saw working were rapidly changing the colour from a weather-beaten grey to a shining aluminum.

We visited the burying ground of the Pope family who were light keepers there foe many years. There are six stone slabs the oldest of which informed me that Edward Pope died July 2, 1871 aged eighty-two years and that his wife Grace died July 10, 1873 aged eighty years. I climbed to the top of the lighthouse and searched the room on each landing in the hope of learning more about the Popes. The most recent date on the stones in the little cemetery was 1899 and I judged that the family must have left almost immediately after that date because there is evidence of the lighthouse as having been occupied by one L. Lemieux.

He has inscribed his name quite artistically on a large rock at the outermost ledge of South West Point. The date is 1900.

Another stone in the cemetery reads:

In Memory Of

Captain John Edgar Joyce

27 years

Of Carbanear Newfoundland

And crew of the

Brigantine Orient

Lost 22 November 1874

Who are buried as follows:

Joseph Taylor aged 25 years

Stewart Taylor 17 years

Thomas Fitzpatrick aged 43 years

William Clark aged 21 years

Charles Henry aged 36 years

Ambrose Forward aged 20 years

Richard Taylor aged 19 years

I learned later from Marcel Duguay, Placide's son, that there are three generations of the Pope family buried there. But I wonder who buried the poor young Newfoundlanders from the wrecked Brigantine.

Since Grace Pope had been buried in 1873 it was probably her son who watched their ship break up almost on his door step, and then buried the bodies that were washed ashore, the year after he had laid his mother to rest.

Dinner at Placide's house was a crowded, happy, noisy affair because the family and the assistant light keeper, and five workmen of the concrete company brightening up the light house, and Francis, Ovila and I all sat down together. They were very patient and good natured with my attempts to keep abreast of the French conversation, but I missed a lot of it, particularly the jokes which kept everybody laughing at me.

After the meal I called Port Menier by telephone and talked to Flora first, and Graham afterwards. During the evening Placide talked and I listened. He only property at South West Point belonging to the company are a few traps. There is an old tomb slab behind the shed which Placide says really belongs right at his front door. There is a Masonic emblem on the slab. The man died in 1839 but I have not got his name in my notes. I cannot remember why not. Perhaps it had been obliterated.

Florida is Placide's oldest daughter. If I remember correctly, the mother died in the flu epidemic in 1928. I slept very comfortably in Florida's bed. She found herself a couch somewhere else, or sat up all night. I was too tired to worry. I wondered sleepily what she did for a nightdress, because hers was on the bed and her brush and comb on the dressing table. She appeared at breakfast time bright and smiling however, so it appears that my comfort was her happiness and I appreciate it still.

CHAPTER ELEVEN

<u>GALIOTE AND CHICOTTE</u>

I decided to walk to Galiote because the wind and the waves made an early start by boat impossible, the likelihood being that it might blow for three days. I set out happily with a cheerful goodbye wave from all the Duguay's. Francis Boudreau accompanied me a couple of miles on the road and insisted on carrying my haversack. I allowed him to do this although I was better able to carry it than he, and would have preferred to do so, but I let him have his way because I understood Francis thoroughly. Years of training in Menier's service and more years of catering to the whims of company officials and wealthy anglers, have made many of the Anticosti people, both men and women, seemingly painfully servile; but as you know them better you realize that it is a surface servility only, and that immediately below the surface is a hard crust of proud independence and self-reliance that make you chuckle to yourself and sometimes wonder who is outsmarting whom? So I simply played the game as Francis wanted to play it. He had phoned Vincent Apestiguay to come and meet us halfway. I think perhaps Graham had instructed him by telephone to do this. Francis relinquished my haversack and left me as we came out of the woods onto the shore. We shook hands solemnly and I thanked him, after which he turned his back while I continued on my eastward way. I remember the high tide and the smell of distance coming in with the strong wind from the sea; the surf breaking on the rocks, and the spray on my face. I remember a host of interesting companions who stepped out of the pages of my sketchy history and accompanied me for short distances, as my wits went wool gathering.

I thought I could see Jacques Cartier,s ships in the distance on the way over from Gaspe. A little under four hundred years earlier, August fifteenth 1534, Jacques Cartier had passed here and given the island its name. I daydreamed that the tall and kindly Louis Joliet walked beside me for a time and talked of his famous trip down the Mississippi with Pere Marquette. He complained that his French Majesty had not been overly generous in the matter of reward. He felt that many favourites who had accomplished much less than he for the glory of France had received much more for their services than this inhospitable island. He felt that he had been discriminated against because he had been born in Canada. I asked Louis where he had died and where he was buried, but he only laughed at my question and said no one would ever know about that. I wanted to ask him if he had known Pierre Radisson and if Radisson had ever visited Anticosti, but as soon as I mentioned the name Louis disappeared. He disapproved no doubt of Radisson's method of dealing with difficult overlords. He would have disapproved still more if I could have told him about how that same Pierre diverted the flow of northern furs and the wealth that followed, away from the sticky fingers of French Royalty and their minions, and into the eager and just as sticky hands of the company of English adventurers trading into Hudson Bay.

Admiral Phipps sailed proudly by, confident that he would capture Quebec, but he too could have learned from me about the stormy Gulf of St. Lawrence and the still stormier governor of Quebec. Louis Gamache, a great black bearded giant of a man with a laughing eye came sailing swiftly to the shore in his smart Shallop with the tall mast and the will-o-the-wisp blue light on top, to show me how he had lured vessels to their destruction on the reef. As he turned and sped away again I could hear his laughter in the wind even after he had disappeared in the distance. While fully awake, and not day-dreaming I saw many deer and foxes always a common enough sight anywhere on the Island. Dozens of seals slopped around in the water or sprawled on the rocks, no doubt disturbed by reports of the latest tactics of the fishermen who were killing the mother seals to take the pelts of the unborn young. Once I saw the elk and his mate from Port Menier. This jaunt around the Island was not such a rare treat for them as it was for me , yet I felt as though I were meeting familiar acquaintances in a strange land, and I was disappointed that they did not seem to recognize me. The lady elk had actually visited our shed in Port Menier in her hungry search for garbage goodies. She had pranced around in the dead of a winter's night on a large square of tin that had fallen to the floor, while her stately mate, unable to follow on account of his magnificent antlers, stood guard in the moonlight atop a great snow-drift almost on a level with our second story bedroom window, from where Flora and I excitedly watched the midnight drama.

Vincent met me soon after I had passed Black river. He had boiled a kettle and made some tea and heated some canned duck in a frying pan. Oh, that ducs! Except for some tripe which I once ate in England, I cannot remember anything else which I ever ate or drank that made me so horribly ill. Vincent was a much better walker than I –it is his business-and as I did not crave his company at any time, or he mine for that matter, but particularly in my misery after the duck, I refused to compete with him in walking, and again surrendered my haversack and told him to go on ahead which he seemed glad enough to do. I recovered somewhat as I resumed my walking but much of the enjoyment had gone. My heels blistered in my rubber boots for one thing, so my thoughts were not as care free as they had been.

I arrived at Galiote about seven o'clock. It had not been a bad day's walk. It is fifteen miles from South West Point to lac Salé-or Great Salt lake- where high tides overflow the shore line to flood the lake with sea water, and six miles from there to Galiote.

At the Apestiguy's house I could not face any food at all, was so tired that even though I went to bed almost immediately and I was awake a lot during the night. Next morning I was still tired and very stiff in all my joints, but remembering a remedy for my kind of sickness which I had often heard of but never tried. I quaffed a glass of sea water and by the power of suggestion I felt better immediately.

Galiote is disappointing even as a salmon stream, and not often rented. Around the pavilion was utter desolation, and inside the house it was eerie and disturbing on account of Vincent's unhappy brood. The desolation seemed to have crept into their minds. I felt a great urgency to escape. The feeling was not by any means the aftermath of what I had come to think of as the poisoned duck.

Poor Vincent's life was much more tragic than that of his brother Joe at La Loutre. I think perhaps Joe's wife made all the difference, as the same inherent morbidity in the two men was the cause of all their family problems. Vincent's wife was short and she may have been pretty and neat and jolly in days gone by but now she was none of those things, poor woman.

We saw much more of this primitive family at a later period when Graham arranged to move them to Port Menier in order that the children might benefit by attendance at the convent school. Perhaps it helped them. Up to the time we left the Island in 1938 the change was not noticeable. When they first arrived in the village they were quite untamed. The oldest boys used to race madly around playing the most inane games that could be imagined, such as swinging on the washing that was hung out on the clothes lines. They made queer screeching noises as they played, more like monkeys than children. Any other children that became objectionable at times, could be caught and reasoned with, but these could only have been caught in a trap, and reasoning with them would have been like lashing the wind. Flora and the older boys used to declare that even the Apestiguy hens were different from ordinary hens and instead of staying near the ground, used to fly high like pigeons and roost on the housetops. On one occasion during the winter time, I was making an inspection of the police station, for some reason which I cannot remember now but doubtless having to do with fire insurance. I was accompanied by Leger Noel, the policeman. The place was cold as a morgue, because it had been closed up since fall. As I stumbled around in the upstairs, lighting matches to guide me, I kicked a strange looking packing case and asked Noel what was in it. I nearly tripped over my own feet when he replied; "Apestigy's baby."

As it turned out, placing the box there until spring seemed to be the best arrangement that could be made in a very difficult and distressing situation, and Graham's consent had been duly obtained.

Such a situation seemed typical of this hapless man. I wonder what in the world became of them all.

After breakfast I checked over Vincent's gear and household equipment, and decided to set out at once for Chicotte. Madame made me some sandwiches which I was glad to have, but Vincent's company I declined. I felt sore all over as I started walking but loosened up with each step. It started to rain heavily when I had gone about three miles, so I was pleased to come upon a cave in the rocks where I could rest comfortably until it had stopped. I had doctored my blistered heels as well as I could before setting out but they still complained rather bitterly, and appreciated the respite and a little additional attention.

At length I got moving again but a lot of the interest had been blacked out by a fog. I could not see very far in any direction. As I rounded a point, I surprised a million ducks who were thrown into a frenzy of excitement at my sudden approach, and quacked themselves into the air in frantic haste. Poor creatures, after the trouble I had had digesting one of their kinsmen the day before, there was no need to hurry on my account.

Eventually I arrived at a cabin which Anselm Poulin used as a shelter in winter time while following his trap lines, so I agreed with my heels to linger again and light a fire. The camp was the typical layout of a careless trapper but I craved tea and thought the place would serve. In the cabin there was a small rusty stove, with a lazy stove-pipe that reached to within about eight inches of the roof. By using his imagination, Anselm had evidently realized the value of having a hole in the roof to let the smoke and sparks escape, but it was evidently too much trouble to extend the stovepipe through the hole. The result was that although some smoke actually went out through the hole, more than enough stayed in, so I changed my plan and went outside to boil my kettle. My fire started very reluctantly with some soaking wet wood from the good ship Galahad of Lunenberg, N.S. which was strewn about the shore at that point. What kind of ship it was, or when or how its last voyage ended on the Anticosti coast could not be learned from its scattered timbers.

Anselm Poulin's young son appeared before my kettle boiled, to escort me to Chicotte, so as it had stated to rain heavily again I abandoned the thought of tea. I ate the sandwiches that Mrs. Apestiguy had made for me, washed them down with water from a creek, and again started walking.

Once during the walk when the fog lifted we saw a large ships steel hull, quite close to the reef. Ocean liners as a rule pass along the north shore and freighters should have been over nearer the Gaspe coast. There was a tremendous sea and I believe that of the fog had not lifted, another ship would have piled up on the rocks. Young Poulin thought so too, and the skipper of the ship must have had the same idea, because he changed his course quickly and he was getting away as fast as he could when the fog closed in again. When next it cleared he was miles away.

We arrived at Chicotte at about four in the afternoon. It was a twelve mile day and I was glad enough to stop early. My heels were glad when it was over.

Anselm was not pleased about the pay cut, but he was not morbid. He had heard about it by telephone and he and his wife had already made their plans for coping with the situation before I arrived. They did no complaining whatsoever to me and they certainly did not allow it to affect their hospitality. Madame Poulin provided me with dry clothes of Anselm's and hung mine in the kitchen to dry. They were a nice friendly family. For one thing they had eight children and I was accustomed to a family just that size. They were happy and chatty as we were at home-perhaps a little noisier than we liked it. I talked to Flora by telephone, and afterwards young Poulin my guide of the afternoon, gave me a bad trimming at checkers. His parents were pleased with him, and I tried to seem pleased too, but in fact I was mortified. The boy showed me a tag which he had taken from a duck he had killed that afternoon. It read:

NOTIFY-BIOL. SURVEY

WASHINGTON, D.C.

I had a wonderful sleep that night under plenty of blankets in a cold room with the wind blowing it at the open window. The next morning broke fine and clear. I was up early and felt completely rested as I dressed in my own dry clothes,

Francis Boudreau telephoned for me to wait
for him at Chicotte , as he expected to be
able to clear S.W. Point later in the day,
and would pick me up in the late afternoon.
I had a nice lazy day.

CHAPTER TWELVE

SHALLOP RIVER-HEATH POINT

Francis was as good as his word and arrived at about five in the afternoon with Kirouac and Hodgson on board. I do not now remember Kirouac or Hodgson but it is not surprising. The swift passing of twenty years has dimmed some memories and obliterated others, yet it pleases me to record their names.

A few miles east of Chicotte is the Riviére du Pavillon, where the French sloop of war La Renommée, 14 guns commanded by Capitaine de Freneuse, was wrecked in a gale on November 14, 1736. The officers, most of the crew, and the Catholic chaplain reached shore safely, but only a few survived the hardships of the winter that followed.

We stopped at about eight o'clock in the evening at Jean Poulin's house at Shallop River, where we enjoyed a beautiful dinner of roast venison. When we first arrived, Jean Poulin himself, standing erect on the shore in the dusk, his features almost as impassive as a wood-carving, had hardly betrayed recognition of us much less given us welcome, but we knew Jean of old, and would have been alarmed for him if he had.

When we had got ashore, and had been introduced to Madame and some bright little girls and boys, there may have been a flicker of a smile of welcome as he poured us all a couple of good drinks of alcohol to warm our insides for the venison. Madame and the little girls where shyly attentive to me, the stranger, but they all chatted happily with Francis and Ovila, discussing the news of the day which they kept abreast of by listening at the telephone.

As to the letter, Jean put it in his pocket and did not deign to open it or make any comment whatsoever. He accompanied me on my rounds and spoke hardly at all, but it was not a strained silence, and there was no hint of ill will. By eleven o'clock we had said our good-byes, and our boat was chattering busily as it carried us along into the night. At first there was a moon but later it clouded over and became extremely dark. About half past one Ovila and I went ashore in a small boat at South Point. Ovila said he could see in the dark, and I had to believe him, because I could not see a thing, and yet we experienced no difficulty getting ashore. The Delisle family was all up and apparently was glad to see even me. Like Placide Duguay at South West Point, Delisle was a federal government employee in charge of the lighthouse. So there were only a few traps of in interest to me. My going ashore was more for curiosity than duty, so that we were soon on our way again headed for Goose Point. Francis had left a message to be phoned to Goose from one of our stopping places, asking the warden there to show a light all night, and he was so puzzled that no light appeared where he thought there should be one. He received a laconic message the following morning when we went ashore at Heath Point which said in effect "out of oil." Francis' stock expression for all such situations was "Oh, c'est épouvantable." (This is dreadful).

The cabin was overcrowded and the air heavy for lack of ventilation so I went outside and stood with Francis in the cold fresh air and watched for the Heath Point Light which finally appeared a pin point of light flickering in the distance. Somewhere on our way that night, in the pitch dark we passed the steel hull of the Italian steamer "Montebello" which had come to a sudden full stop on the reef in 1924, and still sat there perfectly upright as if just sailing into port. It was disappointing to me that we should pass it at night, because I had seen snapshots of it and had counted on seeing the rusty old derelict close up. Perhaps in the desperate search for scrap during WW II, she may have been poured into the prescription for shells and torpedoes, and returned to her homeland as a series of explosions.

At daybreak we were within a mile of Heath Point. The sea was placid and restful and heavy with cold, but there seemed to be much more of it than usual and our boat, the Courcelette seemed to have shrunk.

(Courcelette was also a major tactical objective in the Battle of Flers-Courcelette during the Somme Offensive of the First World War during which the village was razed. The village was assigned as the major objective of the Canadian Corps during that battle and they succeeded in capturing it. Accordingly, the actions and sacrifices of the Canadians are commemorated at the Courcelette Memorial which is just south of the village.)

It was not hard to make-believe that the only dry spot in the world where a dove might find a twig was the little nipple of land which we could see in the early morning light. Were it not for the light-house it could have looked exactly so at the Creation when "God saw that it was good." The rising of the sun was an awesome experience. It seemed that we had come to the very place where it had been resting, and that our noisy approach had aroused it. Despite the fact I was afloat in a small boat in a peaceful country I half expected to hear the roar of guns at any moment. Once, in France, I sat on the rim of a shell hole at day break when no one was awake, no one even above ground except my companion and me, and the silence was deadly. He was a boy from Winnipeg named Code, who was watching the last sunrise he would ever see when suddenly the quiet was shattered by the opening of our barrage and the world in front of us over the German lines was torn asunder. This time there could be no thunder of guns, but there was something so reminiscent of that other time, in the vast quiet, that I wondered what was going to happen this time. Was this perhaps to be the moment of revelation for me, as the other had been for code? This state of significant expectancy was not a new experience, but on this occasion was outstanding because more intense than usual. I explained it afterwards to myself in this way. First, it was Sunday morning and I was not going to be able to attend Mass which was unusual. Secondly, I had been many hours alone with my thoughts the last few days, and thirdly, I had been very tired physically and relaxed mentally. Now was added the spell of this impressive sunrise, and the emotional remembering of an instant out of the past, brought to mind by the quiet of the moment. The sum total was one of those rare and awful moments of insight which sometimes comes to we Catholics during Mass, but this time to me much more vividly than ever before.

In spirit I was attending Mass in a vast cathedral, and in a blinding flash I almost saw the purpose of life and death as God planned it, and for a split-second I almost understood that time does not exist, and at that precise moment I actually was on the hill of Calvary and saw our lord crucified before my eyes and I almost saw why it had to be. I felt as though my mind was about to be permitted a glimpse of God's secret chambers on the other side of life, and I prayed hard as I often do, that my vacillating faith would be strengthened in order that I might pass it on to my sons and daughters none the worse for having been entrusted to me. As always, at the very climax of expectancy, the light went out leaving a deeper than normal brightness like the darkness when I kneel for the blessing and stand for St. John's beautiful but intangible Gospel.

So it was that morning at Heath Point as we anchored the Courcelette, and rowed ashore to a grand breakfast in Rioux's home. Rioux came to Heath Point as light keeper to replace the Bourque family. Two sons of the Bourques had been drowned tragically in 1930. It is not surprising that they wished to leave afterwards. That happening took place the winter that the company had a survey party working at Salmon River, planning a cutting operation that was not carried out for many years. Frolich, a Swedish chap who had a pretty German wife and a terrible nervous stutter, and who I am told rose high in the ranks of Hitler's Storm Troopers later on, was in charge of the party. A few days before Christmas the Bourques learned that an airplane had dropped mail for the survey party near the Salmon River camp. Two of the sons, in their early twenties, travelled on snow-shoes to Salmon River in the hope of finding some Christmas mail there for their family. As it turned out there was just one postal card for them. After a visit of a day or two they set out on their ill-fated journey.

Recently, I checked with Bill Routledge on what really happened. It seems that the first intimation that all was not well was a message from Heath Point to Port Menier via the south shore telephone line, stating that the boys had not reached home. The family could not communicate with Salmon River direct because Fox Bay was the end of the telephone line. For the purpose of the survey and the woods operations to follow (the depression was to be of short duration), the company had installed a point to point radio telephone system between Port Menier and Salmon River. Bill Routledge used to operate the Port Menier end of the system, and at stated hours each day he would establish contact with the survey party. Thus it was that he learned the boys had left for home several days before. He immediately notified Mr. Townsend and shortly afterwards he forwarded an urgent message instructing Frolich to organize a search. Apparently Frolich himself formed a search party of one because for some reason which was never explained to my satisfaction he was unable to obtain volunteers to accompany him. He followed the snow shoe tracks out across the ice of a small bay, until they disappeared. He then took his axe and chopped away at the snow and ice.

After a while a foot appeared and this he tied to his ski. He resumed his chopping and continued until he found the other body which he secured in the same manner. He returned to his headquarters for a toboggan, and still unable to persuade any of his men to help him, somehow succeeded in transporting the two bodies back to his camp site, where they had to remain until spring. Bill made the trip on the toboggan in the spring then, with their two dead sons. He accompanied the party to shelter Bay on the north shore of the St.Lawrence for the burial.

My notes tell me that while at Rioux's house I had a talk with Marshall. It must have seemed important then, but now I do not remember who Marshall was or what we talked about, but again it pleases me to record the fact that we did. I have also noted that the lighthouse was being repaired at the time, and also that it was built in 1835 four years after the one at South West Point.

There is also mention of a very old grave but the note I had on that has been obliterated with wet. I do remember that it was the last record of another shipwreck. I have come to the end of my notes. The last scribble which I have to work from says

"Away from Heath Point about eight o'clock. The day is fine and clear."

CHAPTER THIRTEEN

FOX BAY SALMON RIVER-POTATO RIVER

Wreck Bay having been safely passed, we turned at East Point and started our homeward voyage. Slowly there passed in review before us miles of rocky cliffs the height of which astonished me, even though I had been told about them. I had expected to see the face of Bird Rock fairly alive with gannets like the rock at Percé, but I have since learned that the birds would have been well on their way towards their winter home in Florida, by that date, if not already there. On the map the stream that empties there is called Gannet Brook and the bay is Gullcliff Bay, but I had only heard it called Bird Rock.

At Fox Bay, Fabien Noel and his wife were much upset about the salary cut, and small wonder. They had lived a hard life, and were no longer young. They had a fine large family of sturdy sons and daughters, some of whom were grown up and gone off on their own to seek their fortunes in Québec; others were still growing and needing all the things a growing family needs. Fabien was a competent carpenter and boat builder, but there was no work in his trade so he had to take what was offered and be thankful. Lobster canning was still a relatively important activity at Fox Bay, although there was nothing like the yield that there had been in Menier's time. Even then it had to be tapering off from the much larger quantities canned in the days of Menier's predecessor, an Englishman called Stockwell.

There are stories of cannibalism among shipwrecked unfortunates at Fox Bay that seem to be more authentic than the one about Becsie, but the details are best forgotten. Fabien came down to the boat to see us off. He and Francis had a lot of serious conversation from which I was excluded. Madame came out to wave good-bye. She was a large, capable woman, who hated the humiliations her husband was forced to accept, and she could express herself better in English than I could in French. Of course the messages she gave me verbally to take back to Port Menier were never delivered. The afternoon was foggy and the sea quite rough. As we passed the lighthouse at Table Head, Perry came out in a small boat to take off his provisions, but we did not go in. We turned

in at Salmon River as we planned in to have supper and spend the night there.
Monsieur, Madame and Mademoiselle were at home and extremely hospitable. They made it very easy for me about the letter. The son was away and I am wondering now where he could have been, perhaps visiting relatives on the North Shore. This versatile boy, who had operated the Salmon River end of the radio telephone, and kept good records of the river, had so impressed many visitors who had him as a guide, that he must have been outstanding. All of Anticosti guides were excellent I have never heard a complaint about the guides from either fishermen or hunters, although their praises were varied from warm to lyrical.

I was too sleepy even to be my usual stupid self at French conversation, so I turned in early and had such a wonderful sleep I still remember waking up on Monday morning. I got up early before the family was awake and not wishing to disturb them, stole quietly outdoors and rowed out to the Courcelette in the cold, early morning mist. I washed vigorously, shaved, and cleaned my teeth with sea-water, and then unable to resist the impulse I peeled off my clothes and took a dive in. It was too cold for much swimming but I loved the plunge, and as I paddled ashore again I was so hungry that I pitied the Collards, because the allowance for my meals was fixed by company regulation. They did not seem to resent my appetite however, and served me a wonderful breakfast in a warm kitchen. The sandy beach and the beautiful bay which is called Broom Bay on the map, although I never heard the name in my Anticosti days, make Salmon River a desirable place for wealthy family vacation parties, particularly those not interested solely in fishing.

One such group, with several women in the party fished all the way up the Jupiter, then crossed the height of land and descended the Salmon to the north coast. They took so many salmon on the Jupiter side, that they loved the Salmon River for its beauty alone. The north Shore Rivers are not as good as salmon streams as those of comparable size on the south side of the Island. I suppose there may be a known scientific reason for this. Company authorities in cooperation with the government have had a lot of salmon tagged in the Anticosti streams to aid in studying their migrations. No doubt the study still goes on. In my day they had succeeded in confirming what had been suspected generations ago, that a salmon often finds his way back to the same stream he was spawned in, after a few years in mid-ocean learning how to be a fish. Perhaps by now they have solved the riddle of why he sometimes returns to a different river.

The fog had cleared before we left Salmon River so for hours we chugged westward through a sparkling, choppy sea. The Courcelette knew the way so well she hardly needed steering. All of the boats that Tancrede Girard built had something of his sturdiness and strength of character in them. The cliffs are over five hundred feet high in places but where they leveled off, and at the river openings we could see great expanses of rolling forest where the colors surprised me because in and around Port Menier and all down the south shore we had got used to the unrelieved sameness of the evergreens. What hardwoods were there in the past had been cut down for firewood. Even here on the north side the colors were only a pale imitation of the glorious autumn brilliance of the Laurentian Mountains or the Saint John River but there were enough color-changing leaves to light up large sections and occasionally a patch of rowen trees would hold aloft beacons of bright red berries to illuminate the scene.

CHAPTER FOURTEEN

S.S.Sable

We passed Bear Bay where the best timber on the Island was supposed to be. Perhaps is has been cut since the war. The experts used to say that Bear Bay could be developed into a suitable harbor by building a breakwater, and the year after my trip Adolph Hitler's purchasing agents were eager for a chance to try.

Over towards the north shore of the St. Lawrence, where titanium and iron ore are now in the process of transforming a bleak and almost uninhabitable coast into a thriving hive of industry, in the manner of modern day miracles, could be seen from time to time, ocean going ships seemingly stationary until you realized that they were eerily vanishing from sight and must be moving swiftly. To them the Courcelette creeping along in the shadow of the Island would hardly be visible. Later that day we passed the Vaureal River. I would have made an excuse to stop there if I could have thought up a legitimate one. I would have liked to walk up the river to see

Vaureal Falls which tumble over a cliff several hundred feet high. I have heard enthusiastic estimates of the water power that could be developed there. I doubted these stories because some summers the rivers nearly dry up, and a dried up waterfall would not produce much power. However I missed seeing them and I am sorry.

At Potato River, Ernest Poulin was the man to see. He was a brother of Anselm whose family had entertained me at Cicotte. Here at Potato there was no phone, so news of the salary cut had not penetrated and Ernest was not pleased when he read the letter. If I had stuck a pin in him good and hard it would not have hurt him as much. He made several attempts to speak before any words came, and then came with such a stream of French invective that I was very glad I did not have to try to understand it all, but I certainly got his meaning: Head Office, the Island Manager, and I were equally guilty of the most dastardly conspiracy that had ever been hatched. He classified the various types of blackguards at Head Office, and the short-comings of everyone on the Island. I understood pretty well what made him feel as he did. We had all been through the payout experience several times since the depression started.

I was the messenger that brought the news, and cases have been known where such unfortunates were beheaded. Ernest would have been glad to see my head roll, and in a word, he was not good company and I was not sorry to leave. We passed Charleton Point without stopping, but we were close enough to see people waving to us from the verandah of the house high up on the cliff, and we waved back.

We passed one small motor boat approaching the Island, and several departing. These could have been poachers from the north shore, in fact they almost certainly were. They came for furs and deer-meat and were a constant source of irritation and expense to the company, hungry, unemployed, cheeky humans; who could blame them for poaching?

Their impudence was really outrageous, but there was humour in the situation too. The company, jealous of their rights, naturally tried to protect their property, and forest fires were a hazard requiring constant vigilance, but protecting their rights within the law was a ludicrous performance because happily we were forbidden to shoot our weapons under the feudal system of the hungry thirties.

Sometimes the company men were stopped by poachers at the point of a gun and told to walk the other way. Again, who could blame the wardens for obeying, and perhaps smiling? For their meager pay they risked their lives often enough against the elements without facing the guns of their neighbours from the north shore, who were often their relatives. Perhaps there was a danger of the guns going off accidently, but I doubt it. On the few occasions when poachers were taken as prisoners, to appear before the J.P. at Port Menier as a formality, and from there to be sent to Québec City for trial it was with helpless chagrin that company officials would greet the smiling culprits on board the S.S. Sable a few trips later, returning unharmed and unpunished to their homeland, outfitted with new clothes, their passages paid for, money in their pockets, and sometimes replacements for their traps and rifles better than the confiscated ones.

Dogs were never allowed on the Island, because of the great number of deer and the other animals running wild; but on account of the poacher problem Townsend once obtained permission to import a police dog as an experiment. It was an immediate and complete failure. The dog hearkened to the call of the wild and escaped into the woods with never a backward glance. To relate how he existed there with all creation, beast and human as his enemy, would require the pen, imagination, and knowledge of wild life that the man, Henry Williamson who wrote "Tarka the Otter" had. Reports from various wardens in widely scattered districts came in from time to time, stating that he had been seen in the distance, and the word went out to shoot him. It was never confirmed to my knowledge that the poor lonely fellow was shot, but it was surmised that he died. Perhaps he matched his strength against a bear.

At McDonald River there was more consternation on account of the contents of the letter. The last one was now delivered and I was not sorry. Alfred Martin's wife did all the talking, and said all the things that had to be said. Her opinions coincided with Ernest Poulin's and her fluency matched his. When her husband thought she had gone far enough he held up his hand and she stopped as if he had turned off her oxygen.

The anger which exploded in places where there could be no forewarnings by telephone, and to which I was the unwilling and unwelcome witness, led me to believe that the immediate reactions may have been the same everywhere, only that the first recipients of the news had been able to subdue their feelings before my arrival, and thereby avoid betraying their panic to me. Their problems were all the same; this salary surgery was no more severe for one family than for another; they all had a means of meager livelihood left to them if they chose to accept, or if they chose to refuse, it was understood that transportation would be provided for them and their families and belongings to the north shore or to Gaspe. My report that the payroll changes were unwelcome but in most cases would be accepted proved to be correct. This was exactly what the architects of the plan expected, although they would not have been sorry if they had been wrong.

I would like to be able to tell something about MacDonald, the giant Scot for whom the district and river are called. I am sorry I cannot except to say that he lies buried there not far from Martin's house, and that everyone agrees that he was so obstinate about maintaining his squatter's rights to the land he had settled upon, that he remained until his death to prove his right to be buried there.

That afternoon Francis and I parted company, because while the Courcelette had to go all the way home by water around the North Point and West Point, I elected to walk to Riviere à l'Huile and Trois Ruisseaux, and thence overland to a designated place on the railway line, Princeton, no less, where Graham was having the speeder meet me. Somewhere along about halfway between MacDonald and Riviere à l'Huile in the late afternoon I was put ashore and started to walk. My recollections of the last two days are blurred but I know that I met up with Johnny Francis, according to plan. A tough little man this Johnny, close-mouthed and slyly obsequious so that you wanted to be facing him all the time. He had the name of being impervious to heat, cold, hunger or fatigue. He could sleep in a snow bank on an empty stomach more comfortably than he could sleep at home on a full one. He could write his name in a determined and competent fashion. It came out "Jhony", but it was a perfect signature because it never varied and could not be duplicated like so many signatures could, particularly those made with a cross.

We slept in a trapper's cabin, his I suppose, along the shore. It was quite high up on the hill, and it got very cold during the night but

Johnny did not mind so I pretended that I liked it that way too. In the damp chill of the morning we were walking again as the sun came up behind us and the moon faded out before us. Walking was much more difficult than on the south shore, particularly wading across the mouths of streams where the sand was almost like quicksand and seaweed lay in great beds of soft, smelly slime. Dragging one foot up while the other got lost became a little tiring, and my rubber boots scraped the sore places on my heels, to make the going still more wearisome. I sat down and bandaged them as well as I could and changed my socks. Johnny got so far ahead of me that I walked alone the rest of the way to Trois Ruisseaux. By the time I reached there, I was looking for all the comforts of home and the pleasure of sitting again in my office chair. I had also lost some of my enthusiasm for watching the sunrise, and instead, began to think more about the beauty of the sunsets over Ellis Bay.

No wonder the fishermen liked Isidore Lelièvre as a guide and a cook. When we reached Trois Ruisseaux he had a goose ready for us and I was not too tired to enjoy it although my blanket roll beckoned to me from the corner all through the meal. A few times I dozed off while eating and almost immediately after I had finished I rolled up in my blankets on the floor while my companions did the washing up. The following morning I was a new man. Getting up was not difficult because I was on the last lap of my journey home. I spent a long time preparing my heels for the day's walk, but the going would be much easier because I would not be obliged to wear my rubber boots.

By walking home as I did across country from Trois Ruisseaux to the railway line, I never did get to see Joe Barriault and his family at North Point, or as the map so surprisingly names it Cap de Rabast, but I am more sorry now than I was then. The other places I missed seeing by not staying with the Courcelette did not matter. West Point and Baie Ste. Claire I have already mentioned in my narrative. My walk that day was over familiar ground as I had walked it twice before in the logging days. The trip on the speeder was not a new experience either. In the old days there had been logging camps at Princeton and Lac Simone, the latter named after the popular daughter of one of the logging contractors.

Also, one memorable weekend Flora organized a two-day picnic. The trip was made on this same line with a trailer. We took all the children with us. Patty was the baby then. Nora was there and Bill Routledge and the Lindgrens, the Froliches, Charlie Perkins and Blondie Wright. Blondie was the pilot who crashed at Fox Bay. The first night the rain came down in torrents, but our tents were dry and we had lots of fun singing and telling stories. In the morning we went swimming in the rain. Coffee never tastes as good as it does when made outdoors in the rain. Later that day the weather cleared and we played ball, swam, cooked meals and washed dishes. Mrs. Lindgreen and Mrs. Frolich picked two five-pound lardpails of wild strawberries.

My trip home on the speeder was mostly a matter of hanging on. The track was not as good as it used to be, but the speeder did not go too fast for me that day. The best welcome of the week was waiting for me at home.

CHAPTER FIFTEEN

The German Incident

The year after my trip around the Island of Anticosti, a party of Hitler's Nazis came to look he place over with a view to buying it. Mr. Ellwood Wilson, one of the top names in the pulp and paper industry of that era, accompanied them to the Island and issued detailed instructions for their enlightenment and entertainment.

Doctor Wollert (pronounced "Voolert") a six foot seven professor of the University of Berlin was in charge of the party upon arrival but he did not stay long. He saw to it that his charges were comfortably located in the hotel, and that the bill of fare would be suitable, after which he departed, no doubt to supervise the placing of other such groups.

Herr Wagner ex "Forestiere de l'empereur" a grave middle-age man seemed to be next in seniority. I remember his title in French because that was how he explained what I could not understand in German.

Wagner's closest friend, whose name I cannot recall, was a heavy-set man of middle height bordering on fifty, with greying hair, glowing health and impeccable manners. They were all enthusiastic hand- shakers but this man more than the others. He had been a marine engineer in Hamburg before the war, but he was reduced to peddling fish in Berlin when it was over. He was full of praises for Hitler, which was duly translated into English for us, for having freed him and his family and friends from the clutches of the Jews, and for having set them all down on the road to a better life.

Two others of the group were younger men, say early forties, who seemed to be what we would call public relations men. One of these, Fahrenholtz , Spoke excellent English and French to our knowledge, and according to himself passable Italian and Spanish as well. He was a lighthearted and amusing talker and an accomplished drinker. He spoke in glowing terms of the qualifications of his companions, but when he mentioned "der Fuhrer", there was reverence in his voice.

The other, Herr Muller as he was addressed by his friends, but Mr. Muller as he preferred that we call him, might have been an Englishman or a Canadian as far as speech was concerned. He was an ex-Captain of the German Navy, an amiable and likable man, and his role in the party was apparently to keep repeating how much he admired Canadians, and to relate little anecdotes to illustrate why he did.. There is no denying that we liked his chatter. He found occasions to murmur from time to time during the general conversation on newspaper topics "Mr. Eden is rather difficult."

There was also in this group a rather sinister looking young man, very quiet and unobtrusive who made no apparent attempt to ingratiate himself with anyone either within his own party or with company people. His face was terribly scarred, from, so we were told, sabre cuts from duelling in Germany.

The Kaiser's forester was responsible for the searching enquiries that were made about every phase of woods operations and survey results. The object of the questions seemed to be to confirm information already supplied to them in Montréal. They smirked discreetly at each other at what they saw and heard, and smiled kindly at us. From those who could tell us in English we learned that their smiles were caused by our inept and wasteful attempts to cut wood. The way they told it we were convinced. They pointed out that this was a repetition of what other German missions were encountering elsewhere in our country. After years of depression we found it very easy to believe, and to look forward to any brighter prospect.

The amusement of the group changed to chagrin on one occasion after a trip into the bush on a cruising expedition promoted by themselves. They came back so fatigued that one superman was carried home on a stretcher by the guides, and the others needed two days to rest up. After that trip they named Joe Martin, chief guide of the expeditions "The Man of Iron."

The ex-marine engineer turned fish peddler was the author of the questionnaire on harbor facilities which called for minute data on the depths of water in the Bay and the channel. Soundings were taken under his direction and duly recorded on maps prepared with dots to mark the places.

Then it was enquiries about the soil, about experience with livestock. They even enquired about using seaweed for fertilizer. They did not miss very much.

A few days before Christmas they entertained at a Christmas tree party in the hotel in honour of the ladies, at which they behaved very gallantly, and presented favours to each of their guests. This number one social event was followed a day or two later by a banquet for the men, at which Graham and Watt and several of the top foremen and guides who had been especially helpful, were presented with watches. These were engraved on the back with a map of the Island and the words "Anticosti Expedition 1937." The rest of us each received a large bottle of scotch whiskey. At Midnight Mass five or six of them stood at attention through the entire service, respectfully rather than haughtily, as a gesture of goodwill to the curé and his congregation.

By this time we had accepted them on very friendly terms, and having been persuaded that a change was just around the corner had come to look upon these men as the forerunners of a new order.

On New Year's Eve, Flora gave a party and invited some of them. More came than she had invited, but said they would "wash up" if they could stay. Of course they did stay, and put on fancy paper hats, sang carols, passed drinks and sandwiches, and helped with the washing up. We did not feel like celebrating at all, because Michael had just flown away the day after Christmas with Howard Watt, but our guests were so appreciative we felt we had established ourselves with the new regime. Graham came to our party and contributed some of the drinks. Mrs. Graham had left the Island for the winter.

At the time this group was visiting Anticosti Island and negotiating for its purchase, other parties were being supplied unreservedly with similar information about most of the land bordering on the St. Lawrence River and away to the north   into Labrador, west to Hudson's Bay and south into Gaspe. The aviation companies were all glad to get in on the deal.

"Good- bye, Good- bye", called Herr Knopki a banker and reputedly the moneyman of the expedition, as he climbed into his aero plane, "We shall see you again we are coming back in May." None of them came back of course as they hoped to do, but even if they had come; Knopki would not have been with them because he was killed when his plane crashed.

Perhaps some of them did come back on one of the submarines that pushed their unwelcome black snouts up as far as Metis during the war. But if their purchase schemes did not materialize it was not Mr.Eden who was difficult in that instance. It would seem that M. Duplessis Premier of Québec turned the trick. I used to disagree with theories attributed to M.Duplessis on this subject because it was understood that the Germans were prepared to spend millions of dollars in the lower St. Lawrence. The people down there needed the money. It seemed to me, and to many others that we should take their money and let them come and live here under our laws, but keep them under surveillance.

I have changed my opinion since reading a book about how the conquests of England by Romans and Normans were affected by storming up the rivers of Sussex. I am willing to concede this point and admit that M. Duplessis was the alert watchdog of the nation.

Made in the USA
Middletown, DE
12 August 2023

36600829R00086